Gracious Words

Ordinary Stories That Reveal God's Extraordinary Grace

Belinda B. McKeel

Xulon PRESS

May this
book bring you
blessing & God's grace.

To Loretta

Benard McHale

Dedication

To my parents, Peggy and Sammy Byrum.
You have always been my role models,
my inspiration, and the reason
I know Christ.

Acknowledgments

I want to thank all those who enthusiastically shared stories of God's grace in their lives. Your willingness to give God the glory for his blessings helped inspire me to write this book.

I also want to thank my aunt, Nancy Spivey Turner, who agreed to be my personal editor. Your professional and spiritual guidance is greatly appreciated.

Introduction

If we look hard enough, we can see God intervening in every aspect of our daily lives. He is constantly providing us with real-life situations that teach us about his love and grace. Each one of these stories comes from personal experience or from experiences shared by family and friends. The events recorded in this book are simple and help give us a glimpse of how good God is and how much he wants us to have an abundant life.

Unfortunately, for many of us, today's hectic lifestyle lends itself to less time for reading inspirational literature. I have written this devotional book in hopes that these short, anecdotal stories will enrich your Christian walk. My prayer is that after reading these *Gracious Words* you will begin to see God's extraordinary grace even clearer in the small, ordinary details of your life.

*Yet the LORD longs to be gracious to you; he rises to show you compassion.
For the LORD is a God of justice. Blessed are all who wait for him.*
Isaiah 30:18

Contents

Day 1

$240.00

During a span of about ten months, my mother experienced a series of tragedies that left her near a state of depression. In a short period, she lost her brother, father, sister, and two aunts that left her asking, "What is going to happen next?" It was also during this time that my father suffered a severe heart attack. He was between jobs, and they had no insurance to cover his medical bills. During this same time, my mother and father were taking care of two of their grandsons, and their only granddaughter was staying with them nearly every weekend. My mother is a firm believer that God will not give people more than they can handle, but in this case, she was really beginning to think she would not be able to bear another burden. I believe with all my heart that my father's life was spared the night of his heart attack because God knew my mother would not be able to bear the loss of her husband along with losing the other members of her family. Let me quickly say that my parents never considered taking care of their grandchildren a burden, but sometimes it was a financial strain.

When one of her sisters-in-law became aware of the events surrounding my mother's life, she suggested that my mother accompany her on a trip to Nova Scotia that some of my aunt's friends were taking. My mother told her there was no way she could afford a trip due to the circumstances of the past few months. The largest expense of the trip included an airplane ticket that amounted to $240.00. My mother's sister-in-law told her she would pay for the ticket and they would discuss how my mother would pay her back later.

My mother planned her trip, and she would be gone for ten days. She had never been gone this long, and she was really looking forward to "getting away from it all." Her grandchildren had never gone that long without seeing her and after about four or five days they asked my father where she was and when she was going to come home. My father has always been able to laugh and joke about most situations, and he told the grandchildren that he did not think she was ever coming back.

The morning arrived for my mother to meet her sister-in-law and catch the airplane to begin their trip. Running behind schedule, she left later than she had planned to leave. It was time for the mail carrier, and on her way out of the driveway, she quickly checked the mailbox. After sorting through the mail, she noticed a letter from the IRS. Knowing that this was probably important she took the time to open it. The letter contained a refund check for $241.00. She could hardly believe her eyes. I am convinced that God's hand was all over this incident and it was his way of affirming her leap of faith trusting that he would provide. I also believe God knew she needed to go on that trip and through Divine intervention he arranged a financial plan for her to go.

*Now faith is being sure of what we hope for and
certain of what we do not see.*
Hebrews 11:1

Day 2

1 for 5

One of our local music stores had a sign in the window that said, "Trade in five used CD's for one new CD." I went through the CD's that I did not listen to very much and picked out five that I could part with. I took them to the store and proceeded to pick out my new CD. Most people might think this would not be a good deal, but I did not look at it this way. The CD's I traded in were all non-Christian music and the one I picked out was by the Christian group *Point of Grace*. I began to realize how much more I could gain from this one CD than from the five I turned in. I think it was about this same time that I started listening to Christian music exclusively.

The thing that began to occur to me was that the words to most of the music I had been listening to had no lasting meaning for me. The end of the song meant the end of message, but not with Christian music. Long after the song is over, the message remains. Much like a loved passage in the Bible is meaningful every time it is read; a song with a hopeful message never gets old. In the same way that the scripture is read and placed on our hearts, Christian music is placed on our tongues to bring honor and glory to the one true God and his beloved Son, Jesus Christ.

There is always a Christian CD playing when I am driving, and sometimes I take them to work and continue to listen to them throughout the day. Have you ever been going to work or out to the mall and just before you turned the vehicle off the song that was playing stuck in your head for the rest of the day? Imagine how powerful it would be if the last song you heard was a Christian song with a message that would carry you throughout the day.

Speak to one another with psalms, hymns, and spiritual songs. Sing and make music in your heart to the Lord, always giving thanks to God the Father for everything, in the name of our Lord Jesus Christ.
Ephesians 5:19–20

Day 3

7 O'clock—Until

When we started our women's Bible study, we set a tentative period of 7:00–9:00 p.m. The first few sessions did end close to the two-hour time span, but as we continued to study God's word, we started to ask more questions, share more stories, and spend more time in prayer. Nine o'clock soon turned into 9:30. Before long, we were staying until 10:00 most nights. We could have stayed longer, but most of the women worked and needed their rest.

As the time spent in Bible study increased, the number of participants decreased. Many said they just could not attend a Bible study that lasted so long. What we began to realize was you could not put a timeframe on the Holy Spirit. Sometimes there may be a woman who gets the courage to share something that is heavy on her heart. If we stopped because of what the clock said instead of what our hearts said, we just might miss the only moment she was brave enough to open up to the group. One woman's husband asked her what we did so long at Bible study. She replied, "We have a lot of people to pray for, and there's a lot of stuff in that Bible!" He did not ask again. Another woman commented, "I know you all don't spend all that time talking about the Bible." When I caught the eye of the woman responsible for getting the Bible study started, I knew we were thinking the same thing - "If she only knew."

I will admit I used to think that the 11:00 worship service met my spiritual needs. I then began attending and teaching Sunday school and for a while felt this was meeting my needs as well. Then our women's Bible study started, and I had no idea how hungry I was for God's word. It is amazing what kinds of things can happen when you give the Holy Spirit free rein to work without manmade time constraints. Sometimes I wonder just how many miracles are undone and how many people have left worship services unchanged because there was a specified time to start and end.

Create in me a pure heart, O God, and renew a steadfast spirit within me. Do not cast me from your presence or take your Holy Spirit from me. Restore to me the joy of your salvation and grant me a willing spirit, to sustain me.
Psalm 51:10–12

Day 4

A Penny Saved

Some people consider a "tail's up" penny bad luck. However, I just cannot seem to let any penny stay on the ground. I remember when we were growing up my father always kept a penny jar. When I moved out at age eighteen to attend college, I had to have my own penny jar too. Then one day when I was visiting my brother, I noticed there was a penny jar sitting on his dresser as well. I started to wonder if this was a genetic trait.

For me there is something rewarding about saving a large jar full of pennies and then counting them to see how many dollars I have saved. When I returned to school in my late thirties, money was tight, but I still had my penny jar. One year I bought my Christmas tree with the pennies I had saved. Other times I have used my pennies to help pay for a summer vacation. Nevertheless, I think the one thing I will never forget is the night my daddy went to his dresser and rolled pennies so I would have gas money to return to college. I drove a Volkswagen and with the price of gas in the 70's I could go pretty far with a couple of rolls of pennies.

I once heard a saying that went something like this: "Any gift is expensive if it costs everything you have." Many times, when I was growing up, my parents gave me everything they had, no matter the monetary cost. Their willingness to do without certain things helped teach me the meaning of sacrifice and putting other's needs before your own.

Jesus sat down opposite the place where the offerings were put and watched the crowd putting their money into the temple treasury. Many rich people threw in large amounts. But a poor widow came and put in two very small copper coins, worth only a fraction of a penny. Calling his disciples to him, Jesus said, "I tell you the truth, this poor widow has put more into the treasury than all the others. They all gave out of their wealth; but she, out of her poverty, put in everything— all she had to live on."
Mark 12:41–44

Day 5

Advanced Placement

The term "advanced placement" identifies courses that offer a greater challenge to students who have the ability to meet the demands of extra assignments and more in-depth study. These students have proven themselves during the previous school year, and the teacher's signature validates that they are able to meet the demands of the class. Interestingly enough, this term came up in one of our women's Bible studies.

A friend of mine and I were discussing how bleak and emotionless some people are when they worship God. They do not smile; they feel too inhibited to raise their hands to God; and shouting hallelujah is definitely out of the question. Being a Christian should involve showing joy, gladness, and praise as outward expressions of our love for God and his Son Jesus Christ. I have even heard some Christian pastors and inspirational speakers talk about how important it is to practice how to praise God here on earth because that is all we will be doing in heaven.

One of the women in our Bible study has reached the point in her spiritual walk where she is able to show these outwards expressions of praise without any inhibitions. When someone has reached this level, it is hard to understand why other Christians are not as willing to show their joy in the Lord. She even commented how difficult it might be for these people when they do get to heaven since they have not practiced. She expressed the desire for "advanced placement" when she reaches the pearly gates so she can continue worshipping in the manner she was accustomed to here on earth.

Through Jesus, therefore, let us continually offer
to God a sacrifice of praise—
the fruit of the lips that confess his name.
Hebrews 13:15

Day 6

Against the Law

It never ceases to amaze me how some people let insignificant details fester within the church. I was visiting a friend, and she was telling me about some issues that had become topics of debate within her church and how it was affecting the members. From what I could gather, things were beginning to get out of hand. People were sending negative letters, and there was talk of separating the Sunday school class where some of the comments and suggestions were coming from. I told her that Satan was really enjoying the havoc within their church because the things she shared with me surely did not come from God.

People in the church sometimes get so caught up in the order of service, songs that are sung, instruments that are played, and the way people dress or wear their hair, that they are missing the big picture. I just want to look at these people and say, "You just don't get it do you?" All of their attention seems to be on the messenger instead of the message. It is no wonder that an outsider looking in would not want to be a part of such a group. The most effective way we as Christians can win others to Christ is to live like Christ. I wonder how many people do not participate in church because of arguments among the congregation. On the other hand, many faithful church members have probably left a particular church because of this same problem. Negativism is a tool of Satan and the sooner we learn that the better.

The Israelites proved that man could not abide by the written law given to Moses. That is why Jesus Christ came to usher in the new covenant between God and man. All we have to do is love him with all our heart, soul, mind, and strength. Following all the other laws will be less complicated.

For what the law was powerless to do in that it was weakened by the sinful nature, God did by sending his own Son in the likeness of sinful man to be a sin offering. And so he condemned sin in sinful man, in order that the righteous requirements of the law might be fully met in us, who do not live according to the sinful nature but according to the Spirit.
Romans 8:3–4

Day 7

"Alter" Call

Once every year we have a youth Sunday where the young people in our church are responsible for various parts of the worship service. In the past, they have been in charge of the special music and taking up the offering. One year we decided that the youth would be responsible for the entire service, including the sermon. They all did an awesome job and the service could have not been any better or more Spirit-filled.

To make sure everyone's name was listed correctly, the church secretary faxed me the bulletin so I could proofread it before she ran copies for the Sunday service. Everything looked to be in order except for one small detail. At the end of our worship service, we have an altar call for all who wish to come forward and pray. The secretary had made a typographical error and typed the word *alter* instead of *altar*. I hesitated before being so quick to point out the misspelled word. Then I asked myself, "Was it really an error?" When we get on our knees before God aren't we there to *alter* our lives?

To get the proper definition of the word *alter*, I went to the *Webster's* dictionary. It means to "make some change in." Even though I thought it would be interesting to leave the word spelled as it was, I let her know about the typo, and she made the correction. Now when I see "altar call" listed in the bulletin, it reminds me that not only do I need to go to the altar and get on my knees before God, but I also need to *alter* some things in my life so I can be a better example and help lead others to Jesus Christ.

The Spirit of the Lord will come upon you in power,
and you will prophesy with them; and you will be
changed into a different person.
1 Samuel 10:6

Day 8

Background Singer

I had attended a women's conference and was listening to the CD I had purchased at the event. Every time I get a new Christian CD, I play it repeatedly—in the car, at work, and at home. (Just ask my children.) I was listening to my new CD at work one day when one of my co-workers called to ask if she could meet with me to review a project I had been working on for her. I continued to listen to my CD even though I knew she would be coming soon. However, I turned it down, not wanting the music to interfere with our conversation. I must admit that I also turned it down because I did not want to force someone to listen to something that he or she might not be interested in or opposed to hearing.

It was not long before she arrived at my office. I had the CD case lying on my desk, and when she sat down, she immediately noticed the cover. At the same time she saw the cover, she heard it playing in the background. She exclaimed, "I'm singing on that CD!" I responded with a puzzled look on my face, first because of her claim to fame, as well as my previous intention to turn it down so she would not have to listen to it during our meeting.

The reason for our meeting was put on the back burner, so to speak, so I could hear the rest of her story. She had attended the same women's conference that I had just attended, but in a different city. During the time she attended, the conference organizers had made a live CD. They had told all those in attendance that they would be heard in the background with the singers on stage. We shared our experiences at the conference and both of us acknowledged that we had been blessed by attending with thousands of other women at this particular event.

I felt ashamed that I had almost avoided this conversation with a Christian sister because my intent was not to impose my beliefs on someone else. God quickly got my attention when he made me realize that every encounter is an opportunity to invite a non-believer into the kingdom or an opportunity to share in his unending grace.

"If anyone is ashamed of me and my words in this
adulterous and sinful generation,
the Son of Man will be ashamed of him when he
comes in his Father's glory with the holy angels."
Mark 8:38

Day 9

Called

I have often heard of experiences where people were *called* to become a missionary or a pastor. I wondered how they knew they had been called. Did they have a dream where God came and spoke to them as he did for many prophets in the Old Testament? Was it as dramatic as Paul's conversion on the road to Damascus, or was it through subtle hints that helped them know God's purpose for their life? I would say many people are waiting for a dramatic entrance from God to help them identify their calling. If that is so, then many people are missing his purpose in their lives.

Our church was in need of someone to assist with our junior and senior high youth. I received a phone call from the pastor asking me to help. I made several excuses as to why I could not fill this position and did not think any more about the phone call. I received a second phone call from another church member asking me to help with the youth group. Again, I said I simply could not obligate myself to this ministry. After the second phone call, I began to feel a little guilty, but I still did not say yes. Then I received a call from one of the most respected women in our church. She asked me to help with the youth group, and I began to recognize that these phone calls were not going to stop until I said yes. As I reflected on the events that led me to begin helping with the youth ministry, I realized it was not the people in our church calling me. It was God. He did not come in a dream or blind me with a bright light to get my attention. He used simple strategies to help me see where he wanted me to serve. (I am not so sure that his techniques would not have gotten a little more drastic if I had not accepted after the third phone call.)

After I agreed to help, I confidently told myself that surely I was equipped to help teach others about Jesus. I had grown up in a Christian home, had attended church regularly for most of my life, and my Biblical foundations were strong. What happened next was an unexpected surprise. As I began to teach and attend retreats with the youth group, I saw Jesus with a new perspective. He was not only calling me to help lead others to Christ, but he also wanted to lead me closer to him as well. I have since tried to become more aware of God's plan for my life. By staying in the scriptures and speaking to him daily in prayer, I am keeping the lines of communication open so I do not miss the plan he has for my life. We all need to be searching for his purpose in our lives and be able to recognize all the hints he gives us.

And we know that in all things God works
for the good of those who love him,
who have been called according to his purpose.
Romans 8:28

Day 10

Center Court

One of our former church members is a basket-ball coach for a local high school team. He is not afraid to let others know that he is a Christian, and he uses every chance he can to help lead young people to Christ. Being in a high school environment gives him plenty of opportunities to witness.

He had started a tradition of meeting with his team at center court for prayer after all games whether they had won or lost. Each young man was given the opportunity to participate without feeling obligated to do so. After one game, the team met at center court as they always did. Someone in the stands noticed what was going on and felt it was wrong for the coach to be leading prayer at a school function. They promptly complained to the administration.

The coach explained to the team what had happened and told them that he would no longer be able to meet with them at center court at the conclusion of their games. After the next game was over, the young men looked at one other and seemed to be at a loss as to what they should do. One by one, they moved toward the middle of the court and got down on their knees to pray. This may not have surprised the coach so much, but what happened next did. As the coach was standing on the sidelines, he noticed that members from the opposing team were also gathering at center court along with his players. I think he was probably glad he was able to witness this awesome event from his vantage point instead of being in the middle of the team with no view at all. Coaches always want their players to learn the skills necessary to participate in their given sport. This coach had begun to teach his players skills that would last a lifetime.

My son, do not forget my teaching,
but keep my commands in your heart,
for they will prolong your life many years
and bring you prosperity.
Proverbs 3:1–2

Day 11

Christmas List

When my children were old enough to write, they began to leave their Christmas lists in their stockings by the fireplace. One day when I was searching for an item in my keepsake jewelry box, I ran across some of those lists I had saved. The things they had on their lists were typical items that any small boy would ask for. Their lists included video games, action figures, guns, and sports equipment. Some lists even had lines drawn through items where they had changed their minds. These are precious to me and I especially love the ones that have stars beside the things they really wanted. I would tell them to do this so if Santa Claus did not have enough toys for everyone, he would know what things they wanted most on their list.

You can judge how fast a child grows up by the things they put on their Christmas lists. As my sons grew older, their requests became less toy-oriented. Instead of guns, they would ask for clothes, and in place of action figures, they would ask for gift cards to their favorite stores. This was a sign of independence that told me they could now start making their own decisions. The one item that really told me my oldest child was growing up was the Christmas he asked for an electric razor. I could not believe that I was not down the toy aisles or the local video store hoping and praying that I could find the only thing on my child's list—the hottest video game or action figure on the market.

No matter how hard I tried to grant these Christmas requests from my children, I could not help but think how much more God wants to give us the desires of our hearts. We do not have to make a list because he knows what we need before we ask. All we have to do is get on our knees and present our requests to him. He does not always give us want we want, but he does provide us with everything we need.

"Which of you, if his son asks for bread, will give him a stone? Or if he asks for a fish, will give him a snake? If you, then, though you are evil, know how to give good gifts to your children, how much more will your Father in heaven give good gifts to those who ask him!"
Matthew 7:9–11

Day 12

Commitment

I cannot remember a time in my life when I have not wanted to lose weight. It has always been a struggle for me. What I have found is that to lose weight you have to be committed to the task. You have to set a goal and work towards it every day. If your willpower is strong enough, you will probably begin to see results in a few days. Once you lose the weight, you must then be committed to keeping the weight off. This is probably the hardest part of the process. Getting there is easier than staying there. My mind sometimes plays tricks on me when someone says, "Haven't you lost weight?" Some part of my brain then tells me to go ahead and eat whatever I want. That is when I really have to be strong and continue to eat sensibly and exercise regularly.

Wanting to be a Christian can be similar to wanting to lose weight. Many people want to lose weight but are not willing to change their eating and exercise habits. Many people may want to become a Christian or even a more dedicated servant, but some are not willing to let go of those things that keep them from making a total commitment. You will probably have to give up some things in your life that are not Christ-like. Once you give up these vices, you have to stay committed and not return to your old habits. If you want to become a better Christian, you have to make a commitment to want to be like Christ. Of course, none of us in our earthly state will ever be like Christ, but we can spend our time and energy trying to emulate his character.

The uniqueness of Christianity is that if we do return to our sinful nature, Jesus will forgive us and we can start all over. We do not have to work off our debts; we just have to ask for forgiveness and be sorrowful for our shortcomings. Each time we fall back, we can become more committed to his will and his work. Just as people will notice you have lost weight, they will start to notice your Christian lifestyle as well.

Commit your way to the Lord; trust in him and he
will do this: he will make your righteousness shine
like the dawn, the justice of your cause
like the noonday sun.
Psalm 37:5–6

Day 13

Dragonfly

I am amazed and thankful for the gifts that God has given me. One of the most amazing gifts is the way I can work with my hands. It seems that just about everything I try to do that involves good hand-eye coordination comes easily to me. Whether it is playing the guitar, basket weaving, crocheting, painting, or even typing, I have little difficulty getting my hands to maneuver the objects. I am quick to let people know that it was a gift given to me at birth. For the past several years, I have been making jewelry, which involves a great amount of hand-eye coordination, strength, and patience. It is something I love to do, and it is a great work-at-home job.

Up to this point, I have designed various items. Some include hearts, fish, butterflies, and various shapes such as swirls and triangles. One particular night, I was trying to recreate a design that I had seen in a jewelry-making class. As my fingers manipulated the wire around the pegs on the jig, I noticed that the design I had intended to make was not what I was seeing. As I worked the wire, I noticed that I had created a design that looked like an angel. A few of my friends purchased them to wear as pendants and earrings. One day at work, I saw a woman who had purchased one of my angel pendants. She stopped me in the hall to show me she was wearing one of my designs. I looked at her pendant and noticed that she had it on backwards. She quickly said, "No it isn't. When I wear it this way, it looks like she's praying!" To my surprise, I noticed she was right. What an unexpected gift from God.

I am always trying to come up with new creations, and recently I began making dragonflies. When I showed one of my friends at church my latest design, she commented that she thought the dragonfly had some sort of special meaning or symbolism. I told her that I really did not know about any special symbolism associated with the dragonfly, but I would do some research to satisfy my curiosity. I discovered that the dragonfly is a symbol of Christianity. The dragonfly is born underwater and lives in the dark before rising into the light. When it first emerges, it is colorless and transparent until the sunlight brings out its glorious colors. They are considered symbols of Christianity and remind us that we are to become changed creatures by the light of Jesus Christ.

The dragonfly has become one of my most requested items. Moreover, when I tell people that they are symbols of Christianity, they are simply amazed. We are all human, and some more than others need daily reminders to stay focused on Christ. I need these symbols to help remind me what my ultimate goal is here on earth—to be the hands and feet of Jesus. When I told a woman the story behind the Christian symbolism of the dragonfly she had just purchased she said, "I need all the symbols I can get."

"You are the light of the world. A city on a hill cannot be hidden. Neither do people light a lamp and put it under a bowl. Instead they put it on its stand, and it gives light to everyone in the house. In the same way, let your light shine before men, that they may see your good deeds and praise your Father in heaven."
Matthew 5:14–16

Day 14

Dress Rehearsal

There is a great script, and a powerful man is directing. There are many parts in this great play and a special part has been written just for you. In fact, you are the only one who can play this part. There are many chances for you to rehearse your lines. Sometimes there are moments when you will cry. At other times, there will be some comic relief. You can be sure that at certain moments of the play the audience will be on the edge of their seats. There may be a tragedy written into your part. You will work on your part every day. If you forget your lines, there is a special place you can go to review what you are supposed to say and how you are supposed to act. It is the Bible.

That is just what our life here on earth is—a dress rehearsal. God is watching from above, seeing that we have all the tools needed to play our assigned part. Many times, he allows us to redo the scenes until we get it right. These are the times when he is testing us. Sometimes you may feel like asking God a few questions. You may want to ask, "Are you sure you want me to play this part?" Alternatively, you may ask, "Don't you think someone else could probably do a better job than me with this particular part?" There is nothing wrong with asking questions. This is a great way to begin communicating with someone. Asking a question will usually get you an answer, which can lead to more questions and more answers.

If our lives are dress rehearsals for the great play that will take place in heaven, what kind of review do you think God would write about how you have played your part so far? The greatest review would be him simply saying, "Well done."

His master replied, "Well done, good and faithful
servant! You have been faithful
with a few things; I will put you in
charge of many things.
Come and share your master's happiness!"
Matthew 25:21

Day 15

Faith Floats

One day a carpenter was working on his prized possession. He was designing a boat and he worked at his craft every day with painstaking diligence. Every piece of wood was perfectly measured and cut to the specifications of the pattern. Any board that did not pass inspection was replaced. The carpenter took his time with this project because he cherished every strike of the hammer and every stroke of sanding. The project was nearing completion, and a neighbor stopped by to check on his progress. "Everything's going great" he said "She's almost finished." A few more weeks went by, and the boat was completed. The carpenter stood back and admired his creation. Months went by and his neighbor came to visit again. He asked, "Aren't you going to put the boat in the water?" "Not yet," the carpenter replied. The neighbor asked, "How will you know if it will float if you don't test it in the water?" The carpenter replied, "Oh, I'm sure it will float."

God was up in heaven working on one of his prized possessions—man. He worked at his craft with painstaking diligence. Every muscle, bone, and hair was strategically placed. God took pride in his project because he cherished every breath and heartbeat that went into his creation. His project was nearing completion, and an angel stopped by to check on his progress. "Everything's going great,"

God said. "He's almost finished." The angel noticed some of the attributes that God had given his creation. He had given him a mind to make decisions, a spirit that could live forever—even after his body had died—and the gift of hope so man would never lose sight of all the things God had planned for him. "What about faith?" the angel said. "Aren't you going to give him faith?" "Faith," God said, "is not something I can give him; it's something that has to develop with time and experience." "How will you know when man has attained faith?" the angel asked. "I will know man has faith when he has been tested in waves of trials and waters of temptation and he still trusts in me to accomplish all the plans I have for him. The only way man will know his faith is strong is when it is put to the test, much like the boat that Noah is going to build in the near future."

By faith Noah, when warned about things not yet seen, in holy fear built an ark to save his family. By his faith he condemned the world and became heir of the righteousness that comes by faith.
Hebrews 11:7

Day 16

Father Knows Best

The Bible teaches us that we are supposed to love and fear God at the same time. God loves us, but disciplines us when he needs to. This discipline is only for our own good. If God just sat back and watched us as we made mistake after mistake, we would just grow further away from him and his plan for our lives. This concept was difficult for me to grasp until I started to see the attributes of God in my earthly father. I love him and have feared him at the same time. He was a tough disciplinarian, but only when it was needed to help me mature into a productive member of society.

I was having "one of those days." Nothing in particular was wrong, but I just felt awful. My family would describe me as being "ill." I can describe it in two words—hormonal imbalance. It seemed like I was in a cloud of despair that was weighing me down. My friends always know when I am not feeling my normal self. I stay secluded and do not talk very much. (Some would consider this a blessing at times.)

I was still having these feelings of gloom and doom when later that evening I called my father. As soon as I heard his voice, my demeanor changed. I was talking to someone who loved me and has always wanted me to have everything I needed. Just hearing his voice was comforting and calming. We can all experience this same type of comfort by calling on our heavenly Father. We might not be able to hear an audible voice, but we can rest assured knowing that he is always listening, always loving us, and always has our best interests in mind.

The Lord is near to all who call on him, to all who call on him in truth. He fulfills the desires of those who fear him; he hears their cry and saves them.
Psalm 145:18–19

Day 17

Follow the Signs

When driving, I cannot help but notice how following road signs help us in our Christian walk. For example, when we see a "yield" sign, it should remind us to put others' needs before our own. Christ showed us many times how we should be a servant to all because those who take this path will be great in the kingdom of heaven. When we yield to others, we follow the example set by Christ.

A "no u-turn" sign tells me that if I have been in a situation that does not bring honor and glory to Christ I should not return to that place. No matter how many times we are tempted to return to our sinful ways, we can find strength in the Holy Spirit to keep us from turning around and falling back in sin. As long as we do not make that initial turn to revert to a sinful past, we can keep heading straight on the path that leads to Christ.

One sign that everyone sees most every day is a "stop" sign. This bright red sign should remind us to stop whatever it is we are doing, saying, or thinking if it goes against the will of God. Stopping before we are caught in the clutches of sin keeps us from regretting something we say or do. However, if we are not able to stop before the sin is committed, we have a Father with an unlimited supply of grace.

Probably my favorite is the "one way" sign. It reminds me that there is one way to get to heaven and that is through Jesus Christ the Son of God. Every time I see a "one way" sign, I mentally turn it so the arrow points toward heaven to remind me about the one way I should be traveling. If our trip consists of constant prayer, continuous Bible study, and Christian fellowship, we can stay on the road that leads to everlasting life.

Jesus answered, "I am the way, the truth, and the life. No one comes to the father except through me." John 14:6

Day 18

Found in Translation

A friend of mine who works as a school nurse in our local school system had encountered a Spanish child with multiple disabilities. The boy had experienced a grand mal seizure at school and needed to go to the doctor for a neurological examination. The family was unable to speak or understand English. Susan desperately wanted to arrange for a translator to be present during the doctor's visit so the mother could understand what the doctor was going to tell them.

She made several phone calls and tried to arrange for a Spanish interpreter to accompany the family to the doctor. She contacted some of her co-workers, but they did not know of anyone who could help. She tried to find help in the community, but her attempts there failed as well. Although she could not locate a Spanish interpreter, she was still not willing to send this family into a situation where there would be little or no communication. Susan decided she would go to the doctor's office and be with the boy's family, since she was somebody they knew and trusted. She thought that even if she used some type of sign language, it would be better than nothing.

The day of the doctor's visit arrived and Susan showed up at the medical facility to be with the family. Upon entering the waiting room, something drew her eye to a young man who was sitting alone.

51

The only seat left in the waiting room was directly behind the man who had caught her attention. The mother and child arrived at the doctor's office and came over to sit with Susan. The young man that Susan had noticed got up and came over to where they were sitting. He introduced himself and told them he was there to help in any way he could. He explained that he was the boyfriend of the home health nurse who regularly took care of the child's medical needs. The home health nurse knew that the family would have a difficult time if no could interpret for them, so she had asked her boyfriend, who spoke fluent Spanish, to go and be with the family. He stayed with them for three hours. This is an awesome example of how God is always working a plan to meet our every need.

He who oppresses the poor shows
contempt for their Maker,
but whoever is kind to the needy honors God.
Proverbs 14:31

Day 19

Glowing in Glory

I had the privilege of delivering the Sunday message at my church in December of 2003. It had been a desire of my heart to do this, and the Lord made it happen. When I talked to my pastor about speaking in church, he told me he had prayed to God about who he should ask to speak when he went on vacation. He said God told him to ask me. After I finished speaking, many people said some very thoughtful things to me about the topic I had chosen. One girl told me that if I was not talking to anyone else that day I was definitely talking to her.

One of the members of our congregation came up to me after the service and handed me a note. It was the greatest compliment I had ever received because it said that he could see the glow of the glory of the Lord on my face. You cannot imagine what an honor it was for someone to say that he or she actually could see how much I loved Jesus by just looking at me. It reminded me of one of the songs that we used to sing in our church when I was a child—*Let Others See Jesus in You.*

That same evening, on the way home from church, I stopped at the local convenience store for some coffee. The young man behind the counter politely asked, "How are you doing?" "I'm fine," I said. His reply was something like, "You sure are!" I think my jaw dropped because he quickly said, "I'm not trying to do anything but just to tell you that you do look fine." Did you notice that earlier I said the "young" man? He was probably in his late twenties. I ask you, "What would someone like this see in a woman in her late forties?" He was very kind and continued to tell me that he was only giving me a compliment and did not mean anything else by his remark.

As I got in my car to drive home, I thought about what had just happened. Earlier in the day, a man had given me a note telling me that he could see the glory of the Lord on my face, and now a young man was giving me a compliment that caught me off guard. Here is my conclusion. The man at the convenience store had not seen me; he had seen the glory of the Lord in me. Of this, I am totally convinced and to God I give all the praise.

I have seen you in the sanctuary
and beheld your power and your glory.
Because your love is better than life,
my lips will glorify you.
Psalm 63:2–3

Day 20

God Forgives and Forgets

A mother was washing her son's clothes and checking his pockets for any miscellaneous items. She pulled out a mysterious piece of paper, and when she looked closer, she realized that it had something to do with drugs. She confronted her son, and he was very angry that she found it. She tried to use the opportunity to discuss how dangerous drugs were and hoped he would take her advice.

She then put the paper in her jewelry box. Every time she would go into the box to get an item for herself, she would see the paper she had found in her son's pants pocket. She did not know why she put it there. Perhaps she would use it sometime in the future against her son, not unlike a couple that endures an affair and one keeps bringing it up to hurt the other.

She kept the item in her jewelry box for many months and picked it up several times to throw it away but always put it back in the box. Then one day it occurred to her; she had no reason to keep an item that represented a painful moment from the past. Her rationalization was that God does not keep a record of our sins and she should immediately throw away the evidence. Aren't you glad that God forgives and forgets? Once we ask for his forgiveness, he does not keep a record of our sins and he certainly does not treat us as we deserve.

He will not always accuse, nor will he harbor his anger forever; he does not treat us as our sins deserve or repay us according to our iniquities. For as high as the heavens are above the earth, so great is his love for those who fear him; as far as the east is from the west, so far has he removed our transgressions from us.
Psalm 103:9–12

Day 21

Holy Appetite

One day at work, I received a phone call from a woman who represented a prominent publishing company. She wanted to know if I was interested in purchasing materials for our church youth group. I am always looking for ways to enrich the lives of our young people, and I told her I would be glad to look at any catalogs she had. She then began to describe different types of teaching aids available to help youth leaders. She told me I could preview the materials and decide if I would like to purchase them later. We agreed on several items, and she said they would be shipped immediately.

As we continued to talk, it was not long before I felt as if she were an old friend. She began to tell me how her day had begun. Every phone call she had made was a rejection. Either the people did not want to buy what she had to sell or they could not afford any new materials. She was feeling a little frustrated since her job involved doing the work of the Lord. She had taken a walk during her break time to pray and talk to God about the task.

She said that God had spoken to her in the following way. She imagined herself preparing a table of food that would be tempting to any appetite. Each dish would be seasoned perfectly and there would be enough for all who wanted to eat. She could even have people come and sit around this glorious feast. The only thing she would not be able to do was make them eat. It would not matter how good the food was if they were not hungry. This gave her a new perspective on her mission. She was doing her part, and if people were not hungry enough to take what she was offering, she should not feel like a failure.

She expressed to me how important my job was as a youth leader. She then told me whenever she got off track and things did not seem to be heading in the right direction she always went back to the things she learned in her youth group for guidance. No matter what happened in her life she could always refer to the lessons she learned as a member of a church youth group. This gave me even more incentive to do as much as I could to help the youth in my church and their friends.

"Blessed are those who hunger and thirst for righteousness, for they will be filled."
Matthew 5:6

Day 22

If I'm Not There

When my children were young, I would always let them know what time I would be picking them up from school, ball practice, or church activities. Sometimes I would run late and I would always tell them, "If I'm not there, I'm on the way." By telling them this, they knew I would be there soon to pick them up. When they got older, they would usually finish my sentence for me. I would say, "If I'm not there," and they would say, "We know Mom, you're on the way." Even though I would jokingly act as if I was offended that they were mocking me, deep in my heart I was comforted to know that they knew they could count on me to be there even if I was running late.

Our women's Bible study group had studied the story of Mary, Martha, and Lazarus. Lazarus was sick and Mary and Martha sent word to Jesus to come and heal him. Jesus was only two miles away from where they lived and could have traveled the distance in a short time. They believed with all their heart that Jesus was the Son of God and had the power to heal all illnesses. When Jesus heard that Lazarus was sick, the scriptures say he stayed where he was. In the meantime, Lazarus died.

Jesus did indeed arrive, although it seemed too late to Mary and Martha. He raised Lazarus from the dead and because of Jesus' timing; many people were able to witness the glory of God. Sometimes I have the same feelings as Mary and Martha. Then I realize that Jesus' timing is perfect and he comes at a time when the glory of God will be revealed to many. So now, when I pray, I can hear Jesus telling me, "If I'm not there, I'm on the way."

Then Jesus said, "Did I not tell you that if you believed, you would see the glory of God?" So they took away the stone. Then Jesus looked up and said, "Father, I thank you that you have heard me. I knew that you always hear me, but I said this for the benefit of the people standing here, that they may believe that you sent me." When he had said this, Jesus called in a loud voice, "Lazarus, come out!" The dead man came out, his hands and feet wrapped with strips of linen, and a cloth around his face. Jesus said to them, "Take off the grave clothes and let him go."
John 11:40–44

Day 23

Jesus to the Rescue

During one of my mother's church trips, the bus had engine trouble. The oil pressure was low, and the driver stopped to get some motor oil. They poured it in and when they drove off one of the men noticed all the oil had run out. They pulled the bus into a large parking lot and began contemplating what to do next. Their destination was Pennsylvania, and they were in Virginia.

As they were sitting in the parking lot, a man with long hair and a long beard drove up in a pickup truck. The trip was during Easter and the man was playing Jesus Christ in a local passion play. He asked what the problem was, and the men told him about their engine trouble. He said his church had several buses and they would be more than welcome to use one to continue on their trip. He also told them he would have their bus towed to a service station to get it repaired so they could continue on their trip without being late. He went even further and told them that if their bus was not fixed on their return, they could drive the loaner bus home and return it at their convenience.

They unpacked their broken down bus, placed their luggage onto the loaner, and proceeded on their way. When they arrived in Pennsylvania, my mother called my dad and told him what had happened. She described the entire situation as being a miracle. She said Jesus himself had come to the rescue. My father replied, "Jesus always rescues us when we are in trouble." My mother's reply was, "Yes, I know, but this time he showed up in a red, "King" cab pickup truck."

For he has rescued us from the dominion of darkness and brought us into the kingdom of the Son he loves, in whom we have redemption, the forgiveness of sins.
Colossians 1:13–14

Day 24

Just Believe

I have always been amazed at how the advertising industry can convince people that their product will do what is says it will do. I have tried some of the products I have seen advertised, and some have worked for me. On the other hand, I have tried other products that did not live up to the promises made. As a teenager, I was overweight, and I remember seeing ads on television and in magazines that said if you took a particular pill or drank a special liquid you would lose weight. I tried some of the products that I saw advertised and none of them lived up to the promises made in the advertisement.

Many people still spend millions of dollars on products that do not live up to the promises made by the commercials. We seem to be ready and willing to believe things that seem unbelievable. Some of the other advertisements that seem unbelievable to me are the ones that say you can get rich quick by purchasing certain advertised books or videos. I have always figured the reason some of these people are self-made millionaires is that so many people purchased the books or videos they were selling.

On the other hand, the things that people find hard to believe include understanding that Jesus can love them in spite of their sins, that he came to earth to die just for them, and that he can forgive any sin committed except for blasphemy against the Holy

Spirit. Jesus tells us that all we have to do is believe in him and his heavenly Father. Those who believe will receive. We will receive mercy, grace, forgiveness, love, and everlasting life. His promises are worth believing and his guarantee can be found in scripture.

I write these things to you who believe in the name of the Son of God so that you may know that you have eternal life. This is the confidence we have in approaching God: that if we ask anything according to his will, he hears us. And if we know that he hears us—whatever we ask—we know that we have what we asked of him.
1 John 5:13–15

Day 25

Kaleb's Violin

My father has a passion for music. Some people cannot turn away a stray cat or dog, and some have a talent for rescuing struggling flowers or plants. He cannot bear to see an instrument not being played. He frequents yard sales most every weekend, and many times he comes home with an instrument. It does not matter if he or anyone else in the family can play it; he just wants to give it a chance to make music.

One day he came home with a violin that had the marks of being quite valuable. The person he purchased it from said it had been in their family for many years. He tried to research its origins and found that it was probably hundreds of years old. Even though no one he knew could play it, he took the violin to a local music store to have it repaired.

We had started a praise band in our church, and one of our youth who decided to join the group played the violin. I shared this news with my father, and one day when I was visiting, he sent the violin back with me so Kaleb could play it. My father wanted someone to play the violin so he would know its quality. Every time I talked to my father after I returned with the violin, he wanted to know if "that boy" had played the violin yet. I told him he had and Kaleb liked it more than his own violin. In fact, it sounded better than the one he played in his school orchestra.

We arranged for my mother and father to attend our church when our praise band was leading the worship service. They wanted to hear Kaleb play the violin. After the service was over, I introduced Kaleb to my father. They bonded immediately because of their mutual love and respect for fine musical instruments. My father told Kaleb he could keep the violin. He later commented that there was no way he could take that instrument after he had played it so beautifully. Kaleb's mother came to me and insisted that my father not give the violin to her son. Her reasoning was they would buy the violin instead of accepting it as a gift. She did not understand that when Kaleb played the violin to the glory of God the price was paid in full as far as my father was concerned. Incidentally, this violin was the second one my father had purchased and given away.

About a year later when my father was making the yard sale circuit there happened to be another violin for sale. The man had purchased it in hopes that he would learn to play it, but as it so often goes, he never did. My father had now purchased his third yard sale violin. When one of my father's friends asked him if he wanted to sell it, my father quickly replied, "No, the Lord told me to give the first two away, but he told me to keep this one."

Kaleb's mother took the violin to a music store to have it appraised. After a close inspection, the storeowner told her the neck had been removed and replaced and because of this, the violin had lost its value. She quickly responded, "No, it hasn't." The storeowner said, "What do you mean it hasn't lost its value?" She explained how the violin had made it into her son's hands. He understandingly said, "I guess you're right."

My father did learn how to play the violin. One day while he was practicing my mother came down the hall and said, "I can name that tune." He was playing *Where We'll Never Grow Old.*

It is good to praise the Lord and make music
to your name, O Most High.
Psalm 92:1

Day 26

Lewis' Legacy

My father's parents had eight children—five boys and three girls. Many years ago, it was common for newborn children to die from a variety of illnesses. However, in the case of my grandparents, their first child died from the burns he received while my grandmother was trying to start a fire in their wood heater. His name was Lewis, and the family mentioned his name from time to time. The burns on my grandmother's arm were a constant reminder of his birth and eventual death at fourteen months of age.

There are many questions in our lives and only God knows all the answers. How could God allow someone's firstborn child to die from this type of accident? Why does it seem like some of the most dedicated disciples of Christ suffer more than what seems to be their share of misfortune? Why do some people recover from cancer, and others lose courageously fought battles? I am sure for every person who reads this; there could be a different question, which seems to have no answer. Sometimes God does provide answers to our most difficult questions. It may be that he reveals his plan to us in a short period. Many times, it is years before we can begin to understand the answers behind some of life's most difficult questions. I know for myself, he has shown me how his plan is working in my life, but I still have a few questions that have no answers.

In the fall of 2004, we celebrated my father's seventieth birthday. At the end of the meal, my father stood up to thank everyone for coming and celebrating his birthday. Each birthday has been special since 1993 when he had a massive heart attack and did not expect to live through the night. As he began to talk, he reminisced about his early life, his children, his wife, and his extended family of brothers, sisters, nieces, nephews, and grandchildren. There was a common theme; it was love. He said he remembered his eighth grade teacher making everyone in the class memorize the thirteenth chapter of I Corinthians and recite it in front of the class. He surely did not understand why she made them do this, but in retrospect, he came to appreciate what she was trying to teach them along with all the other things they were learning in school. He also remembered having the words "Best Loved" under his senior picture in the high school yearbook. Of all the titles given to the senior class, he was proud and humbled by having the best title anyone could get.

He went on to talk about the love that had been so present in our family throughout all the years of ups and downs, good times and bad times; years of prosperity and years of financial uncertainty. He summed it up by going all the way back to Lewis. He said he believed that after his mother lost her first-born son, she then held onto each child closer and loved them even more because one never knows when that chance will be gone. Even though I never heard her mention the details around Lewis' death, I feel certain that she carried a tremendous amount of guilt by somehow feeling she was partly responsible for his death. My dad believed that Lewis' death was one of the main reasons that our family had been so close all these years.

On the way home that day, I reminisced about all the things he had said. The one thing that kept running through my thoughts was the fact that the death of one was the cause of so much love. Then I thought about God losing his son. Because of Jesus' death, we are bound even closer in the family of God. The early Christians had to hold on tightly and love each other even more because their teacher and perfect example of love was no longer in their physical presence. I am thankful for my earthly family; because of them, I am a part of God's family. As painful as it is, even death can be rationalized as a bad thing that happens for a good reason.

"For God so loved the world that he gave his one
and only Son, that whoever
believes in him shall not perish
but have eternal life."
John 3:16

Day 27

Lifting Hands

I had always seen people lifting their hands in praise during worship services, but I had never felt comfortable doing it in public. Nevertheless, I had reached the point where I could lift my hand while I was driving when I was listening to a particularly emotional Christian song. I shared this with my friend, and she told me she lifted her hands in praise one day when she was driving, too. I immediately pictured a vehicle speeding out of control, but she told me she was sitting at a stoplight when it happened.

I had recently been to a women's praise and worship conference and noticed some of the women lifting their hands during the singing. Even amongst eight thousand women, I still could not lift my hands in praise even though I totally understand what it meant and why the women felt so uninhibited. I do not know if this was difficult for me because of what I thought other people might think or just because I had not reached this spiritual part of my journey.

The next Sunday after the conference, we were all back in our church of about two hundred people. It is quite a culture shock to move from clapping, shouting, and dancing in a worship service to one that is a little more subdued. As I stood during the benediction, I felt as if I were going to explode with emotion. Then I lifted my hands because I felt the need to give an outward sign of praise to honor God and his Son Jesus. Then the most amazing thing began to happen. It felt as if electricity was flowing down into my hands and arms, and giving me a "holy rush." I truly believe I felt the Almighty Power of the Holy Spirit that day and that the feeling I was experiencing was his Holy Presence. I now anxiously await each opportunity I have to lift my hands to give him the honor and praise he deserves.

Lift up your hands in the sanctuary
and praise the Lord.
Psalm 134:2

Day 28

Like Mother, Like Daughter

I feel sure that most young girls want to grow up and *not* be like their mother. I know I did. Something happens around the age of thirteen that makes a mother seem like the dumbest person on earth. As adolescents, we all thought our mothers worried too much. That is until we had children of our own. We could not understand why our mothers did not like the clothes we wore, the way we cut our hair, or the friends we had. Most young girls would say that their mom was just old-fashioned and not "with it."

As I grew up, I often told myself that I would never do or say some of the things my mother did or said. For a while, I accomplished just that. Then like a force that I had no control over, I slowly began to pick up some of her quotes and mannerisms. For example, she has always said, "It's better to have it and not need it, than to need it and not have it." I wish I had a dollar for every time I have heard that one. No matter how hard I tried to suppress what was happening I could not stop this slow transformation. Many of these characteristics began to show up after I had children. My husband noticed this change and every once in a while, just to make me mad, he would say, "You sound just like your mama."

As I grew older, I realized what a remarkable woman my mother is. She always puts others' needs ahead of her own, and she goes out of her way, almost daily, to help someone. I remember her saying to me that she felt like her day was not complete unless she had helped someone else. Her life has truly been one of a servant, whether it was serving her husband, her children, her church, or her friends. The woman that I had tried so hard not to be like was the very person I wanted to be. I have a ways to go before I develop her characteristics, but now when my husband tells me I sound just like my mama, I tell him that is one of the best compliments anyone could give me.

Children, obey your parents in the Lord, for this is right. "Honor your father and mother"—which is the first commandment with a promise— "that it may go well with you and that you may enjoy long life on the earth."
Ephesians 6:1–3

Day 29

Listening for God

I have often wondered why, in the Old Testament, God made himself known in such powerful ways. He appeared to Moses as a burning bush, led the Israelites as a cloud, came to many in vivid dreams, and even had a wrestling match with Jacob. I suppose since the events in the Old Testament were before Jesus' birth, God had to show himself in these remarkable and miraculous ways. Maybe these mighty glimpses of him helped the people believe in his power.

I have never heard anyone describe God appearing to him or her as he did to people in the Old Testament. I have heard some people talk about experiences where they caught a quick glimpse of him or heard him speak to them in a human voice. The realization of God interacting in my life is that he so cleverly talks to me through other people's voices. It is most remarkable. I know that this has happened to me a number of times. I did not know it was God talking to me until weeks, months, or even years later. If you draw near to God, he will draw near to you, and then you can really begin to hear his voice.

One particular incident that my father described to me is what I would call a great example of how God speaks to us, even if it is through the voice of a child. After graduating from high school, my father enlisted in the air force. His four-year commitment was approaching, and he had to decide whether he was going to reenlist or if his life was going to take another turn. He would drive home every weekend and pass his mother and father's house before he would get to his own home. He always had to stop there first. One reason was obvious; it was his first home. The second, third, and fourth reasons were his two nieces and his nephew. They had been abandoned by their father and my father's sister had to move back home with her three children. My father had become their "father figure." He said that they must have had an internal clock that could tell the exact time he would be driving up the lane because they were always outside waiting for him. As he approached the house, he could hear them shouting, "Uncle Sam's home, Uncle Sam's home!"

After this happened a few times, he knew what decision he was going to make about his future. There was no way he would reenlist in the air force and not be able to make it home on weekends. These children needed a father. I believe the excitement in their voices was actually God talking to him. I wonder how many times God has tried to speak to us, but we were not attentive enough to get the message. One thing I do know is that when I am about to make a big, life-changing decision, I try to listen for his voice to find out what his will for my life is. It is not always an easy thing to do, but through prayer and spiritual discernment, we can actually hear the voice of God leading us and guiding us through all situations.

"My sheep listen to my voice; I know them,
and they follow me."
John 10:27

Day 30

Litmus Test

Some people may wonder how they can tell if they are living a life that is pleasing to God. Jesus taught that the two most important ways to please God are to love him with all your heart, soul, mind, and strength. Then love your neighbor as yourself. Following these two commands makes your life pleasing to God. If you feel you still need affirmation that your life is producing spiritual fruit, you can ask yourself some key questions. Actually, the process could be similar to a litmus test.

A litmus test has an either/or answer. It tells whether something is acidic or alkaline. A Christian litmus test can also tell you if your life is acidic or alkaline. Because I have forgotten much of the science, I temporarily learned in high school, I went to the dictionary to make sure I understood what the results of a litmus test indicated. According to *Webster*, an acidic reading means something is sour. An alkaline reading means that something is able to neutralize acid and form salts. This made me think of what Jesus said about Christians being the salt of the earth. Our lives should change the flavor of the world, not blend in.

Some key scriptures can help you answer these two questions. "Is my life pleasing to God and is there any evidence to show—specifically—spiritual fruit?" In Paul's second letter to Timothy, he talks about how difficult it will be to stay on the Christian path during the last days. Paul says there will be boastfulness, prideful behavior, brutality, and conceit. Children will be disobedient to their parents. He also says people will be unforgiving, ungrateful, and unholy.

Take any of the characteristics listed in the paragraph above and simply place your name with the act. Am I being boastful or prideful? Am I unholy or unforgiving? Am I ungrateful? You can give yourself your own litmus test to find out what type of results you will get.

"You are the salt of the earth. But if the salt loses its saltiness, how can it be made salty again? It is no longer good for anything, except to be thrown out and trampled by men."
Matthew 5:13

Day 31

Looking for Guidance

When I was a young girl learning to play the guitar, I used to sit opposite my father so I could see his hand on the neck of the guitar. It was from this angle that I could see the finger positions for the chords. I trusted in his ability to guide me with the correct techniques. When our family would get together to play music, I would always sit where I could see his hands so I would know what chords to play. When my oldest son began to play the guitar, he would sit opposite me and watch my hands so he would know what chords to play next as well.

At a recent family gathering, I was sitting opposite my daddy while other members of the family joined in a circle to play music. One particular song was giving me a difficult time. My daddy actually stopped everyone and said, "Belinda hasn't gotten it yet, let's stop so she can get it right."

As I reminisced about the early years with my father, I could not help but smile, knowing that after all that time nothing had changed. I still looked to him for guidance, knowing he would not lead me in the wrong way. Then I began to think about my son. He may not always ask for guidance, but I am compelled to set a good example for him. When we are seeking guidance in our lives, we need to sit opposite Jesus, or more appropriately, at his feet, so he can show us the right and true path. He will always show us the way and sometimes he may just have to stop everything that is going on around us so he can get his message across.

"Listen, my son, accept what I say, and the years of
your life will be many. I guide you in the way of
wisdom and lead you along straight paths.
When you walk, your steps will not be hampered;
when you run, you will not stumble.
Hold on to instruction, do not let it go;
guard it well, for it is your life."
Proverbs 4:10–13

Day 32

Loyal Fan

During my youngest son's junior year in high school, the football team had a tremendously successful season. They had worked hard and were undefeated going into the final game with a 15-0 record. The students, faculty, and the entire community were pulling for them to go all the way and become state champions. The team they were playing had won the state championship three years in a row, but it did not dampen the spirits of the football team and their faithful fans.

Flags were flying, and the fans traveled to a local college campus in support of the football team. I was not able to attend, but I anxiously waited to hear the final score. The game was played late on a Sunday night, so I did not get a chance to see the score until Monday morning. There it was in bold print. It was the fourth straight championship for the opposing team. At first, I thought how disappointed the losing team must have felt to make it all the way to the finals and lose their only game of the season. Then I thought what an honor to be able to play in such a game. Many high school football players and other athletes as well, never get that chance.

I finished getting ready for work and as I pulled up to the stoplight, passing in front of me was a car with my son's school flag flying proudly. I thought—what a loyal fan. Even though the team had lost, they were proud to let everyone know whom they had been pulling for, no matter what the outcome. We practice, plan, and pray for outcomes in our lives. Sometimes we feel like winners, and sometimes we feel like losers. I have a fish license plate on the front of my vehicle that tells others I am following Christ. When facing contests that are usually of the spiritual warfare nature, I sometimes come out on the losing side. (This is only because of my own weaknesses.) However, when I get ready to get in my car, I do not get a screwdriver to take off my license plate because I just do not feel like being loyal to Christ that day.

The most important time to let others know you are a Christian is when life is tough. Following Christ in the valleys can be our greatest witness. No matter what circumstances are surrounding our lives, it is comforting to know we serve a God who is in control of the entire universe. Our human minds cannot understand his divine plan, but we can rest assured knowing he has a plan, a perfect plan. For all of you who are running the race for Christ I say, "Play hard and pray harder."

Everyone who competes in the games goes into strict training. They do it to get a crown that will not last; but we do it to get a crown that will last forever. Therefore I do not run like a man running aimlessly; I do not fight like a man beating the air. No, I beat my body and make it my slave so that after I have preached to others,

I myself will not be disqualified for the prize.
1 Corinthians 9:25–27

Day 33

Not Lucky—Just Blessed

When I worked as a schoolteacher, one of my students was involved in a serious car accident. The boy was six years old, and he and my son were in the same class at school. One afternoon he had crossed the road in front of his house to check the mailbox. When he was crossing back, a car hit him. Some reports said his shoes landed 50 feet from his body. The ambulance took him to the hospital, which was just two miles from his house. He had a couple of broken bones, but his main injury was being in a coma because of head trauma. He woke up a few days later, and my son and I visited him in the hospital.

While I was in his room, I talked to his mother, who was a minister, about how lucky they were that he survived. She quickly said, "Oh, we're not lucky, just blessed." It was about this time that I stopped using the word "lucky" so much. I could hardly believe my ears when she told me the story her son had told her after he woke up from his coma. He said he remembered flying towards earth with an angel on each side of him. He also said he could see the earth from far away as the angels flew him safely back to his home.

I had read books about people having encounters with angels, but this was the first time I had heard a firsthand account. I truly believe that this little boy was indeed telling the truth and it was just not his time to die. The Lord was gracious to this precious little boy and his family. His life was spared because his time on earth was not complete.

For it is written: "He will command his angels concerning you to guard you carefully; they will lift you up in their hands, so that you will not strike your foot against a stone."
Luke 4:10–11

Day 34

Of One A-"chord"

In the fall of 1993, a couple in our church lost their son in a tragic car accident. They wanted to do something special in memory of their son. One of their close friends was the pastor's wife, and they had been talking about buying a set of hand bells for the church. The couple decided to purchase these bells as a memorial to their son, Robbie. Sue, Robbie's mother, recently shared with me that the cost of the bells was exactly ten percent of a financial settlement she received soon after Robbie's death.

The pastor's wife gathered a group of eager women to play in the hand bell choir. I was fortunate enough to be one of those women, and it was a joyful feeling to play in memory of my friend's son and to the glory of God. We continued to play the bells for about five years. When the pastor and his wife moved to another church, we packed the bells in their cases, where they remained silent for the next five years. People in the church were praying that someone would come forward to lead the hand bell choir.

The Lord spoke to me and told me that I was the one to lead the hand bell choir. I have very limited musical training, but I do have a natural ear for music. This is a precious gift from God that is evidenced by many in my family. Since I felt the Lord calling me into this new ministry, I felt I needed to give up one of my other duties in the church. About this same time I was reading a book by Max Lucado titled *Learning to Have a Heart Like Jesus.* In one of the chapters, Lucado talks about finding the place where you are most productive. He ended the paragraph by saying we should take a few irons out of the fire so the ones we leave in can get hot and accomplish God's plan in our lives. I admire Lucado's writing, and I felt as if I had been set free to give up one of my church activities. I then began to pray for someone to take my place as the youth leader. I had someone in mind, and I prayed for God to touch her heart so this other plan could transpire. I waited for just the right moment to approach my friend about taking over my job as youth leader. She was very receptive to the idea. I immediately began recruiting and making plans for our first hand bell practice. There was a buzz within the church. "The hand bells are going to play again" was a common phrase heard from the congregation. No one was happier than Sue, also a member of that first hand bell choir.

The first practice was scheduled, and to my surprise, thirteen people showed up. Two more had said they wanted to play but could not make the first practice. This was my first clue that God was all over this endeavor. I explained the process that we would be following for playing the bells. I chose a simple, familiar song from the hymnal for beginners and was almost a guarantee to be successful. After a few practice rings, we settled down and began to play. The song was a series of chords. A chord is three or more tones sounded simultaneously. The chords we were playing involved nine to ten tones played at the same time. What happened next could only be described as God dwelling among us. We had five women in the group who had never played hand bells, but from the sounds coming out of that room you would never have known it. Each played with precision and rang the bells to the glory of God. After finishing the song, we looked at each other as if to say, "Did we do that?"

Overwhelmed by the success of our first practice, I almost ran out of music to rehearse because the group was such a quick study. I started to think about how we had come together on that Sunday afternoon to do the work of the Lord. The success of our hand bell practice was evidence that when all are working toward a common goal, you can achieve great things. We gathered with one purpose—to play in harmony for the glory of God. Imagine if all activities in the church could be this successful. It is possible when we focus on why we are here and that we are to use our God-given talents to bring honor and glory to his name.

Therefore if there is any consolation in Christ,
if any comfort of love, if any fellowship
of the Spirit, if any affection and mercy,
fulfill my joy by being like-minded,
having the same love, being of one accord,
of one mind.
Philippians 2:1–2 (NKJV)

Day 35

Overflowing Cup

The twenty-third psalm is probably the most well known chapter in the Bible. It is one of those passages that loses it's poetic rhythm when translated into anything other than the King James Version. In just six short verses, David gives us a complete picture of God as a shepherd, soldier, and savior. I remember memorizing it at an early age, but it has only been in my later years that I have come to understand its complete meaning.

The part that says "my cup runneth over" was a mystery to me until I became so filled with the Holy Spirit that I just had to pour it onto someone else. When God is blessing your life in ways that you could have only imagined, you have to share it with someone else. I have several close friends whom I call when God is moving in my life, and they do the same to me. Our women's, weekly Bible study created a group email list so we did not have to wait an entire week to pour out the blessings on each other that God had doused us with since our last meeting. This type of instant gratification is positive and powerful as opposed to the other kinds that seem to consume this generation.

Sometimes people do not always react to the spilling out of the Holy Spirit in a positive way. I have seen the Holy Spirit overflowing from a sister in Christ only to have the person on whom it was spilled react in a negative way. It was as if that person was saying, "Stop! You're getting me all wet." On the other hand, I have seen the opposite response. It is almost as if this person had been in a dry wilderness without any relief in sight. Then the cool, refreshing water of the Holy Spirit makes them say, "Keep splashing, I can't get enough!"

> *Thou preparest a table before me*
> *in the presence of mine enemies;*
> *thou anointest my head with oil;*
> *my cup runneth over.*
> Psalm 23:5 (KJV)

Day 36

Patiently Waiting

During the Christmas season, our youth group participates in caroling for those who are in the hospital, nursing homes, or homebound. It is a Christmas tradition that I wish more people would continue. One Christmas we decided to visit members of our church who were homebound or just needed a special visit because of events that had occurred in their lives during the past year. I asked the church for names of those who wanted us to sing for a friend or family member so we could begin to make plans.

I received names from different church members who knew of people that would benefit from some holiday cheer. I had the names written down so I would not forget anyone. During our first stop, we got a little lost and the evening started out disorganized. However, after a few telephone calls, we finally made it to the first house. We continued until we had visited everyone on the list—or so I thought.

The next day one of my friends who had gone caroling told me about a woman and her mother who had waited for us to come by, but we never showed up. In fact, she was the first one to give me her name for Christmas caroling. I felt so awful. When I thought of her and her mother sitting there, waiting for us to show up, it made me feel like I had really disappointed them. As this incident lingered in my mind, it made me think of Christ's promise to return for us at the appointed time. There will be people living on earth who will get to experience the fulfillment of this great promise. It also made me realize that we humans do not always follow through with the things we say we are going to do, whether it is intentional or unintentional. However, Jesus can be trusted to fulfill his promises to us.

We did return to the house we missed that Christmas, and as a peace offering I took a live Christmas wreath. The women were surprised and since they had gotten an extra gift, they told us they hoped we would forget them next year too!

"In my Father's house are many rooms; if it were not so, I would have told you. I am going there to prepare a place for you. And if I go and prepare a place for you, I will come back and take you to be with me that you also may be where I am."
John 14:2–3

Day 37

Perspective

Just when you think that things are not going so well in your life, God can put things in perspective for you. My son decided he wanted a motorcycle. I felt just like most mothers when their child would ask this question. All I could think about was how dangerous it would be. I remember the first day he rode it in the yard. My son got on, started the engine, and took off around the house. I experienced the same feeling as the first time he rode a bicycle without training wheels. He slowly learned how to ride, taking short trips, and I prayed a silent thank you to God each time I heard him drive in the yard. As he gained more confidence, he decided to ride to his grandfather's house, which was a thirty-mile trip. I really did not want him to go that far quite yet, but as with all new challenges our children have to face, I knew that eventually he would be taking longer trips. I agreed and sent him off with a prayer.

It was on this same night that the men of our church were presenting their annual rendition of the Living Last Supper. The play was almost three-quarters finished when the church phone rang. I have had many phone calls that have brought bad news and when a phone rings, I silently hope and pray it is not for me. After a few of those phone calls, my son would start saying, "You're never going to believe what happened." I asked him never to use that phrase when he calls me. It is amazing how many different things can race through a mother's mind when she gets this type of phone call.

I was quietly watching the play when one of my friends tapped me on the shoulder and told me the phone call was for me. It did not take long to figure out who was calling. It was my son, and he had wrecked his motorcycle. This is when a mother goes through many different emotions. I went from mad, to thankful, to I-told-you-so, to scared, and back to thankful that I was actually talking to my son. A friend drove me to my father-in-law's house to see how bad the accident was. The motorcycle got the worst of the accident, and the only thing that happened to my son was a dislocated toe and some sore spots.

My son would not talk much about the accident as it was a scary, near-death experience. Although, a few days later, he started to talk about what had happened. He misjudged his speed as he was going around a sharp curve and ran off the road. Thankfully, he landed in a field of soft dirt that helped to break his fall. Then he told me something that really was astonishing. He said he saw the whole accident happen seconds before he actually wrecked. I know that God was with him on that ride as most people who have this type of accident usually get seriously or fatally injured. Although he survived, I still had to deal with the fact that repairing the motorcycle was quite expensive and the hospital bills were high.

I was out shopping during the after-Christmas sales that same year when I saw a couple who had a son the same age as mine. I used to drop my son off at their house every morning for a ride to school. She asked me how my son was doing, and I wanted to know what her son had been doing since graduating from high school. The next thing she said hit me like a brick. She said her son died in a motorcycle accident a year earlier. It really put my son's accident into perspective. No matter how much it cost me financially, I did not have to pay the ultimate price of losing my child. I rode home that day thanking God for my motorcycle repair bills, my hospital bills, and for sparing my child in an accident that could have easily taken his life.

Pray continually; give thanks in all circumstances,
for this is God's will for you in Christ Jesus.
1 Thessalonians 5:17–18

Day 38

Plant Now—Harvest Later

Our youth group has had the opportunity to sing at several youth events. Each time they have sung, it has been truly inspirational. However, during practice they have a hard time staying motivated to sing. Some even claim they cannot sing, but the youth leaders know better because they have proven themselves quite talented when performing for hundreds or thousands of people. Our choir director works hard to pick songs that are contemporary enough to keep their interest and to provide a Christian message to the listener as well as the youth themselves.

One night after they had finished practicing, our choir director said, "I wish they felt like I do when they sing." She is also the adult choir director, the church organist, and a member of a women's trio who often sing at our church as well as at other churches in the area. Her ministry is her music, and she puts all her heart and soul into every song. She finds it hard to understand why others are not as passionate about their music when they sing.

One night after a disappointing practice, she looked distraught. She was having a difficult time getting through to them how important their message in song may be to someone in the congregation or the audience. Many times, she has told them the words to a particular song may speak to someone who had never been touched by the Holy Spirit before. This may even happen when everything else in the service fails to make an impression on their hearts. I said to her, "We're just planting seeds and we may never get the chance to see the full harvest."

"But the one who received the seed that fell on good soil is the man who hears the word and understands it. He produces a crop, yielding a hundred, sixty or thirty times what was sown."
Matthew 13:23

Day 39

Playing by Heart, Praying by Heart

Ludwig van Beethoven is responsible for some of the most beautiful musical compositions ever written. However, his life was not so beautiful. His childhood was unpleasant as his father was a strict disciplinarian and an alcoholic. His mother died when he was eighteen and he placed himself as head of the household because he had two younger brothers to take care of. One of the most fascinating facts I have learned is that Beethoven had almost completely lost his hearing during the last ten years of his life. This seemingly unfair turn of events put an end to his performing career, but it did not stop his ability to compose music.

During this period, he continued to write beautiful sonatas and symphonies. He also gained legal custody of his nephew during this time, after a long legal battle. Even though Beethoven showed affection for his nephew, the feeling was not mutual. In spite of these obstacles, Beethoven did not stop doing what he loved. I have tried to imagine how many times one has to play a piano so the sounds of the notes are memorized as the fingers stroke the keys. Obviously, it is many, many times. To be able to continue to play skillfully after one has lost their hearing would be a great accomplishment. To compose music seems almost impossible.

The reason this story touched me is the fact that

just as the notes were etched in Beethoven's memory, even when he had lost his ability to hear, we need to have God's words so memorized in our hearts that we can retrieve them at will. We need to know his word *by heart*. When we lose our *spiritual* sight, it would be helpful to have read the scriptures so many times the words are embedded in our memory. We should be able to retrieve familiar scriptures in the midst of struggles and trials, not only for ourselves, but also for others in need of an encouraging word. One scripture that is constantly on my lips is, *"I can do everything through him who gives me strength"* (Philippians 4:13). Jesus tells us we are going to have trouble in this world (John 16:33), but the next part of this verse is powerful: *"But take heart! I have overcome the world."* When I am struggling with life's difficulties, I remember Paul's words from II Corinthians 12:9, *"My grace is sufficient for you, for my power is made perfect in weakness."*

These are just a few of the verses that I have stored in my spiritual memory bank. You probably have some that are your favorites. I encourage you to repeat these scriptures aloud when faced with obstacles. Beethoven's symphonies were composed of notes that were permanently embedded in his memory. Our symphonies to God can be composed of words that are fixed in our minds and written on our hearts.

*"This is the covenant I will make with the house of
Israel after that time," declares the Lord. "I will put
my law in their minds and write it on their hearts.
I will be their God, and they will be my people."*
Jeremiah 31:33

Day 40

Pursuit of a Dream

Many years ago, I read a book titled, *Do What You Love, the Money Will Come.* It talked about making a living doing something you really enjoy as your source of income. It gave helpful hints for making such a dream come true. The one thing that really stuck in my mind was the fact that, according to this book, ninety-five percent of people are unhappy at work. That tells me that only five percent of people actually enjoy their work and love what they do.

Thinking about all of those unhappy, working people made me think about some of the meetings I have sat in at work. Sometimes I just let my mind wander, and I look at the faces of those around the tables. There is usually not one happy face. In fact, they look stressed and uncomfortable, and they have that, "I'd rather be anywhere than here" look. Then I start to wonder how many of those people are doing something that they love. On the other hand, are they just going through the motions of an unfulfilling job, which seems to have more cons than pros?

There are many ways to make a living, so why not choose something fulfilling and enjoyable? I wonder how many people reading this have a secret dream and never dared to step out in faith and see what might happen. I can think of so many things that a person might want to pursue as a full-time career. The first thing that comes to mind is music. How many gifted musicians are playing to the four walls of their bedroom or living room, all the while secretly imagining that they are performing in front of a live audience? Many people have the gift of painting. Alternatively, maybe someone has always wanted to run for a public office. Someone else may have a gift for cake decorating. Why not start out small and see what happens? I would like to know how many of the well-known people in the world started out doing something that they loved to do, made it their career, and are now household names. (I am sure Paul Harvey could name a few.) I believe there are countless people who fall into categories similar to these. What better way is there to praise God than letting people know the only reason you are able to perform certain tasks is that it is a gift? A casual conversation with a non-believer can suddenly turn into a witness for Christ. All we have to do is ask him how he wants us to use our special gifts he has given us.

I have always loved to work with my hands. For some reason, God gave me the ability to do many different things with my hands. It is the most remarkable thing, and when I am doing something I love, I get into this thing called "flow." Flow means being engaged in something so enjoyable and intriguing that you lose all track of time. Hours may pass by without you realizing the amount of time you spent doing the thing you love. It is amazing how slowly time seems to pass when you are doing something that is not pleasurable.

As I approached and reached middle age, I asked myself if I had met all the goals that I have in life. On the other hand, could there be something more that I may want to do but have not tried? I think it would be so sad to live a life according to someone else's agenda, or never to pursue the dream you had since childhood or maybe from your teenage years. I can honestly say that I have been fortunate to have several good jobs. But recently while I was sitting in one of those meetings, going over the agenda and getting assigned tasks to do, I truly had to stop and ask myself, "Is this the way I want to spend the latter years of my life?" I think the answer is no. I would like for my work pace to slow down a little. It seems to grind on and on as I clock in, clock out, look forward to the weekend, and then on Monday start all over again. The weekends are so packed with the things that I love to do I am almost too tired to go back to my full-time job. Recently, I was talking with a co-worker about this same topic. It turns out that she had a few hidden dreams of her own. She left my office teary-eyed, thinking about a dream that she once had.

You may ask, "How do I know if the dream I am pursuing is my will or God's?" I think one of the best ways to know is if you are running into closed doors or walking through open doors. Recently, I have gotten into a part-time career that is building into something larger than I could have ever imagined. The amazing thing is, it all started because of a woman's Bible study. As I worked to try to start a small business, I noticed that God seemed to be walking before me and setting a plan in place. Many things have happened that seem to be telling me to keep walking through the doors and get ready for what God has on the other side.

One day I was washing my son's clothes and I was going through his pockets to get any paper, candy, or money that he had left. What I found on this particular day was a small piece of paper, with a profound statement on it. It talked about wishes and dreams. He has a big dream of his own and I am sure that it is going to come true for him because he is so passionate and determined to succeed. The note said, "You are never given a wish without also being given the power to make it come true" (Richard Bach). This went where all the other important pieces of paper go—on the refrigerator. I read it nearly every day.

I do not know if God has plans for my part-time business to become my full-time job. However, it is a good feeling to know I have at least tried it and went in pursuit of a dream. This verse was on a daily calendar that I received a few years ago. I tore it out and put it on my bulletin board at work. It gives good advice about how one goes about pursuing a dream and it comes from the wisest man, other than Jesus Christ, who ever lived—King Solomon.

For a dream cometh through
the multitude of business;
and a fool's voice is known by
a multitude of words.
Ecclesiastes 5:3 (KJV)

Day 41

Puzzle Pieces

Our lives are like puzzles. We may have pieces scattered all around without a clue about how they fit together. Then a few pieces begin to fit, and some of life's circumstances begin to make sense. It may be some time before we find any more pieces that interlock. Sometimes we even try to force-fit pieces together, attempting to alter God's plan for our lives. We may even try to leave a particular piece in place before we realize it just does not fit, and we reluctantly remove it from the puzzle. God has the box cover that shows what our lives will look like when all the pieces are perfectly placed. Sometimes I think I would probably mess things up even more if I knew what the final picture looked like.

I have never attempted to put a puzzle together without the box lid, and I do not want to try. In the same way, I do not want to try to put the pieces of my life in place without asking God for his Divine guidance. Only he knows what the final picture will look like, and our job is to rely on his perfect will for our lives to make all the pieces fit together.

In him we were also chosen, having been
predestined according to the plan of him
who works out everything in conformity with the
purpose of his will.
Ephesians 1:11

Day 42

Railroad Crossing

Have you ever been in a hurry to get somewhere when suddenly you hear the train whistle and then see the crossing bars drop? I have always been amused at how quickly people will turn around and try to beat the train before it crosses the road in another part of town. I have tried to do the same thing a time or two. The last time I tried it I was on the way to my hair appointment. (You women will understand my dilemma.) I had an opening where I could safely turn around, and I did just that. I went toward the side of town where the train had not been, thinking I could beat it because it was moving slowly. As it turned out, the train caught me at another crossing. I decided to return to my original spot and wait until the train had passed. As I turned the corner, I saw the caboose crossing the road. I thought about all those detours I had made. They had amounted to nothing except to make me more apprehensive about being late and to burn a little more gas.

The last time the train caught me, I again noticed how quickly people were turning around to avoid being detained. As I sat and observed the situation, it made me realize we Christians do the same thing. God has a perfect plan for our lives. Sometimes he puts detours in our way so his plan will materialize. We then take matters into our own hands, going out of our way to reach our destination. Sometimes all we need to do is sit still and wait for God to raise the crossbar. Think of all the heartaches, disappointments, unfulfilled plans, and wasted time we could avoid if we would just learn to trust God and his plan.

Many are the plans in a man's heart, but it is the Lord's purpose that prevails.
Proverbs 19:21

Day 43

Sleepover

My youngest son had asked one of his friends to spend the night at our house. I told him it would be okay. He called me later to tell me he had invited another boy to spend the night as well. I told him that would not be a good idea because we really did not have enough room. We actually do have room—floor room that is. Boys do not seem to care where they sleep as long as they are with their friends. Later that day, I asked my son if his second friend was still going to spend the night. He informed me that he was and I again tried to talk him out of having an extra friend sleep over.

Realizing that my son's friend had already made plans to spend the night, I knew it would be difficult to withdraw the invitation. My son and his two friends eventually came home and I asked the second boy if he had his extra clothes. He told me he had gotten some dress clothes to go to church the next day. I told him he did not need to dress up and he said he would watch my son and dress accordingly. Then he said something I will never forget. He told me he was trying to visit some churches with his friends since he trusted their judgment. He also told me he had not gone to church as a child and was not much of a believer, but was trying to make some sense out of things he had heard from his friends. You can imagine how small I felt. My son's invitation may have been one of the few chances he would ever have to visit a church and I was trying with all my might to keep him from spending the night.

The church service was special that Sunday morning. The preacher was very relaxed as he tried a couple of different things during the sermon. There was lots of laughter, which I think is a good thing at the appropriate time. The title of the sermon was "Why Be a Christian?" and we even had Holy Communion that Sunday. Things could not have worked out any better. However, isn't that God's nature—perfection?

We took all the boys out to eat after church and the boy that I had tried so hard to keep from spending the night said, "That's the first church I have ever felt welcome in!" By now I was about to crawl under the table because I had almost destroyed this boy's chance to experience God with Christians who accepted him no matter where he was in his walk. God will get his way—if we do not get in the way.

The Lord foils the plans of the nations;
he thwarts the purposes of the peoples.
But the plans of the Lord stand firm forever,
the purposes of his heart through all generations.
Psalm 33:10–11

Day 44

Strong Roots

Few will forget the aftermath of Hurricane Isabel that struck the Atlantic coast in the fall of 2003. Even though many heeded the warnings and prepared accordingly, others underestimated the impact of the storm. I remember watching as the hurricane drew closer, and I began to realize that my parents would probably be in Isabel's direct path. I prayed for their safety and other members of my family who lived along the North Carolina and Virginia coast.

My husband and I headed towards my parents' home two days after the storm was over. I had never seen anything to compare to the destruction that the storm left behind. The closer we got the more damage we saw. There were trees down everywhere and most had fallen on power and telephone lines. Thankfully, we were able to make it all the way to my parents' house. They and my brother were very fortunate that neither of their houses had sustained any serious damage from the storm. Others had lost everything.

After unloading some supplies at my parents' house, we went to clean up the debris in my brother's yard. He lives in the home place, where my grandparents raised their seven children. One of his neighbors stopped by to see if everything was okay, and he commented that my brother's yard looked better than any other he had seen. This was remark-able, considering the fact that eight, large pecan trees surround his house and the branches of these trees usually do not hold up under such destructive conditions.

My father and I were talking about how some trees had fallen on houses, and others had not. In my brother's case, no trees had fallen, and the only things we had to clean up were piles of small branches. My father then remembered that when his sister had lived in that same house, she had always fertilized the pecan trees. He said that was probably the reason why the trees were still standing, and there was no structural damage to my brother's house.

My Aunt Mae died in September of 2001, but her impact on the family was still evident because of her care for those pecan trees. Those trees were deeply rooted in the ground, making them able to withstand hurricane-force winds. When our faith is deeply rooted in the teachings of Jesus Christ, we are able to withstand the storms in our lives that we are prepared for and even those that may come as a complete surprise.

"The one who received the seed that fell on rocky places is the man who hears the word and at once receives it with joy. But since he has no root, he lasts only a short time. When trouble or persecution comes because of the word, he quickly falls away."
Matthew 13:20–21

Day 45

Suffering for Doing Good

The youth in our church never cease to amaze me with their talents, their insights, and their love for God. Our youth group grew rapidly over the years. Most of our youth members were children who had grown up in the church. However, some members of the youth group were just visiting. I do not think our youth were going to school or their neighbors and saying, "Hey, why don't you come to our youth meetings on Sunday nights?" What I think happened is that other young people saw something different in our youth, and they were curious to know what it was and how to get it.

Our church was having its annual youth Sunday. It was indeed a blessing as we watched these young people stand up and claim Jesus Christ as their Lord and Savior. I distinctly remember the words of one of our youth as he gave thanks for his Christian parents. He told the congregation that he had always known who Jesus Christ was and it saddened him to know that many young people have to walk in darkness until someone shows them the Light. I remember a loud "Amen" from the audience; it was his mother.

This same young man had a similar experience with his high school football coach. Our youth participate in many church events that take place during the summer and sometimes it means missing mandatory football practice. When a football player misses a mandatory practice, they have to work twice as hard to make up for the time they missed. I imagine that they are in for some ridicule from the coaches as well. This particular young man's coach approached him and asked why he was willing to pay such a price for attending these youth events. His comment was one of the most profound statements I have ever heard about being a Christian. He said to his coach, "This is going to be my last year of playing football; I'm going to be a Christian for the rest of my life." The coach never asked another boy on the team about missing football practice to attend summer youth events.

If you are insulted because of the name of Christ, you are blessed, for the Spirit of glory and of God rests on you. However, if you suffer as a Christian, do not be ashamed, but praise God that you bear that name.
1 Peter 4:14,16

Day 46

The Bird Lover

My maternal grandmother loved birds more than anyone I have ever known. She had a parakeet named "Pretty Boy" that talked to her and her only. However, there were times when she could get him to say a few words for us grandchildren. I remember riding with my grandmother to go shopping one day, and she almost stopped the car on a dime, trying to keep from hitting a small bird. Many people will do this for a dog, cat, or a squirrel. How many people have you known that would do this for a bird? She had chickens in her yard that produced eggs, but because of her love for birds, she could not bring herself to eat chicken.

As she and my grandfather grew older, they made quite a perfect pair. He was failing physically, and she was showing early signs of dementia. My grandfather was able to help keep her thoughts clear, and she was able to help him do the things he was physically unable to accomplish. So between the two of them they were able to complete most of their daily tasks. We visited more often when their health started to fail, and they were always so happy to see us. I will always remember that every time I went to visit, my grandfather would say, "There's my girl."

During the time that my grandmother started showing signs of dementia, her stepson died of a heart attack; one month later my grandfather died after he had fallen and broken his hip. She could not remember going to the funerals, but there was one thing she could remember—my mother's phone number. After she was placed in a nursing home, she would call my mother four to five times a day and say, "I can't find Stockton; I can't find him anywhere." My mother would try to explain, but it never seemed to help.

During the next summer, my grandmother's youngest daughter died after a courageous battle with breast cancer. When my mother would visit, grandmother would always ask about June and if she was coming that day. My mother relived her sister's battle with cancer repeatedly with each visit. Then she decided to respond with, "June's not coming today" and that would usually be enough to change the topic of conversation. It made both of them feel better. My mother then found a small, life-like bird that resembled some of the ones my grandmother had owned. Holding the bird was comforting to her. In a few short months, my grandmother stopped having conversations during our visits. She had several strokes during her stay in the nursing home, but she was always pleasant. The staff would comment on how they enjoyed taking care of my grandmother because she was so easy going.

She died a few years later, and during the funeral, her youngest son delivered the eulogy. He reiterated the fact that just maybe God had allowed this dementia because he knew her sweet spirit would not be able to stand the heartache associated with the loss of her loved ones. I can just imagine that when she got to heaven and saw my grandfather she said, "I've found him," and he probably said, "There's my girl."

And I heard a loud voice from the throne saying, "Now the dwelling of God is with men, and he will live with them. They will be his people, and God himself will be with them and be their God. He will wipe every tear from their eyes. There will be no more death or mourning or crying or pain, for the old order of things has passed away."
Revelation 21:3–4

Day 47

The Cheerful Giver

As the leader of our church youth group, I was always trying to think of various fundraisers to help our youth participate in as many church-sponsored activities as possible. Our church is supportive of our youth ministry. The number of youth who attend our Sunday night meetings had doubled so fundraising had become a large part of our yearly activities. I knew the Lord would provide in times of need. However, during my years as youth director, I came to understand this truth even more.

An older couple, who did not have any children, had been attending our church. They had seen how active our youth were, and they wanted to help support our ministry. The pastor came to me with a check from this generous couple. I do not know what I thought would have been a sizable contribution, but I was not ready for the amount on the check. This couple gave our youth ministry a check for $7,500.00 and told the pastor to use it for spiritual retreats. They did not want any child to miss an opportunity to grow in Christ because of finances.

This donation was only the beginning. A few months later, one of our church members came and told me she had something for the youth. It was a check for $2,300.00. She made me promise not to tell anyone and that the only one who needed to know already knew—God. She and her husband did not want anyone to know about their donation, as they did not want any of the credit for their good fortune. I promised I would not tell and I did not even tell my husband.

It was not long before my friend told me she had another surprise for me. She quietly saw me after church and handed me a check for $1,500.00. I assured her I had not told anyone about our secret, and she jokingly said if I wanted to continue to receive these checks, I had to keep the givers' names anonymous. I assured her I would keep our secret. Many months went by, and I had not received any money from my friend. Then as I was speaking with her on the phone about an activity at church she said, "I have another check for you!" It was not long before she handed me a check for $1,400.00. Each time she gave me the money she would say, "God's been good."

"Be careful not to do your 'acts of righteousness' before men, to be seen by them. If you do, you will have no reward from your Father in heaven. So when you give to the needy, do not announce it with trumpets, as the hypocrites do in the synagogues and on the streets, to be honored by men. I tell you the truth, they have received their reward in full. But when you give to the needy, do not let your left hand know what your right hand is doing, so that your giving may be in secret. Then your Father, who sees what is done in secret, will reward you."
Matthew 6:1–4

Day 48

The Emperor's New Suit – Revisited

I have always enjoyed stories that have a good moral ending. The Emperor's New Suit, by Hans Christian Anderson, is one of those stories which has several lessons. One is the downfall of materialism. Another is the importance of being honest, and a third could be that sometimes the most truthful statements come from the most unlikely people.

In this story, the emperor is so consumed with his clothes that he spends all of his money on new suits. The story says that he would change his clothes every hour and go out to show them off. Two swindlers came to town and saw the chance to make a lot of dishonest money. They saw how much the emperor loved his clothes, and they concocted a scheme to make everyone in the town believe that they were master weavers who could manufacture the finest cloth that anyone had ever seen. They went so far as to say that this special cloth would be invisible to any man or woman who was not fit for their job, and anyone who could not see the cloth was unpardonably stupid.

The emperor heard about this cloth and not only did he want new suits of clothes made out of this material, he thought it would benefit him greatly in determining the fit from the unfit, and the wise from the stupid within his court. He ordered the cloth immediately and paid the men a large sum of money to get started. Word quickly spread throughout the town about this magnificent new cloth.

The two men bought the finest silk and gold materials money could buy. They hid the materials and then pretended to weave until late into the night. The emperor was curious as to the progress the weavers were making. Since this cloth was so special, and he knew that it would be able to show who was fit or unfit for their office, he decided to send his honest old minister to see the weavers. When the minister got to the room, he could not believe his eyes. He saw nothing at all, but did not say anything. The weavers asked him what he thought of the cloth. After a moment of silence and after remembering what it meant if you could not see the cloth, he quickly told them that it was quite exquisite. This is what he reported to the emperor.

The emperor then sent another honest courier to see the cloth, and soon the whole town was talking about the beautiful material that these two weavers were making. All the while, they were requesting money to buy more gold and silk, which they keep for themselves. The emperor's curiosity got the best of him, and he decided that he would like to see the clothes the weavers were making. When he arrived, he could hardly believe his eyes. He saw nothing and asked himself, "Am I unfit to be emperor or am I stupid?" He then turned to the weavers and told them the cloth had his gracious approval. Everyone who had traveled with the emperor exclaimed how beautiful the cloth was for no one wanted to be called stupid or unfit for his or her office.

The weavers then pretended to take the cloth off the looms and said, "At last, the emperor's new suit is now ready." The emperor then pretended to put on his new suit. Everyone was still admiring the invisible cloth. Once the emperor was ready, he started a procession through the streets of the town. Everyone had come to admire the emperor's new clothes because they had heard what it meant if you could not see them.

Then a small voice came from the crowd. "But he has nothing on at all," said a little child. The townspeople began to whisper about what the child had said. Before long, all the people were agreeing with the child. This made a great impression on the emperor for he thought to himself that they were right. Nevertheless, he tried to keep his dignity, and the procession continued to march throughout the town.

Even though this is a fairy tale, it has many truths that can apply to all of us. There are people speaking against Christianity all over the world. Some are unable to stand up against negative comments and just go along with the crowd. Peer pressure does not just happen in adolescent years. It affects us throughout our lives. We as Christians have to be as honest and as bold as the small child in this story. We have to be willing to speak the Biblical truth. More importantly, we need to know the truth so we can quickly recognize "religious swindlers" whose only goal is to sway public opinion in believing that the ways of the world are acceptable.

---

*For the time will come when men will not put up
with sound doctrine. Instead, to suit their own
desires, they will gather around them a great
number of teachers to say what their itching ears
want to hear. They will turn their ears away from
the truth and turn aside to myths. But you, keep
your head in all situations, endure hardships,
do the work of an evangelist, discharge all
the duties of your ministry.
II Timothy 4:3-5*

Day 49

The Gift of Grace

Our women's group had started a Bible study on grace. As my friend and I were preparing for the first night, we thought it would be a good idea to make each woman a gift bag with scriptures on God's grace to read throughout the week. We typed scriptures on pastel paper, laminated each one, and placed them in colorful gift bags. Each woman randomly picked a bag. The idea began to grow as we then decided that after each woman received her gift bag with scriptures, she would place a small gift in the bag and bring it to the next week's Bible study. Of course, everyone was excited about this idea. Our reasoning was that these gifts would be like God's grace. It is something we cannot do anything to earn; all we have to do is freely accept this gift.

The second night of Bible study arrived, and a few of the women had forgotten to bring their bags with a gift inside. It was obvious to us that the ones who did not bring a gift would be the first ones to choose from the colorful bags in the middle of the floor. The women who had forgotten their gifts did not want to participate, but we insisted. The next week everyone did bring her gift, and we all began to look forward to what was in each bag.

We randomly chose each gift, and we were simply amazed at how many of the women received something that they wanted. Sometimes the gift was something the person needed but did not realize it until looking in the bag. Other times the gift perfectly matched the woman's interests. We began to realize even more how these gifts were symbolic of God's gift of grace in our lives. Sometimes it is exactly what we need, and other times he pours out his grace on us when we least expect it.

And God is able to make all grace abound to you,
so that in all things at all times,
having all that you need, you will abound
in every good work.
Thanks be to God for his indescribable gift.
2 Corinthians 9:8,15

Day 50

The Man in Scrubs

*In memory of Kathryn Bohannon,
sister of Karen Hungate.*

During a particularly emotional night at our weekly women's Bible study, a woman shared a story about the death of her younger sister. Being born only ten months apart, not only were they close sisters; they were best friends as well. The younger sister had just quit her life-long career in chemistry to pursue her dream of designing ballroom gowns. The sisters had recently spent lunch together discussing the details of this new adventure.

The accident happened at a busy intersection. Karen's sister was T-boned by a man who had run a stop sign. The paramedics administered CPR as the ambulance headed for the emergency room. Karen found out about her sister's accident, and she frantically made her way to the hospital. When she arrived in the parking lot, a man wearing hospital scrubs met her before she could get to the door. He said, "You're Karen aren't you?" She said she was and he immediately told her to go to the waiting room and forgive the young man who had caused the accident. She thought this seemed a bit odd, but she went to find him anyway. She was easily able to pick him out among the others sitting in the waiting room. He was obviously distraught, and she assured him that if there was any way to have avoided the accident, she knew he would have done so. During that brief encounter, she forgave him for what had happened and anything that was about to happen.

Karen went back to find the man who had met her at the entrance of the hospital, but he was nowhere to be found. As she described him to the staff, no one seemed to know who he was. She also was never able to make contact with the man who had so gallantly performed CPR on her sister immediately after the accident had happened. As she recalled the events of that day, she was convinced that God had sent earthly angels to help with one of the most difficult experiences of her life. She also believed her encounter with the man in scrubs helped the young man who was responsible for the accident deal with the guilt he was feeling.

When Karen was finally able to see her sister, the medical staff informed her that she was brain dead. The only thing keeping her alive was the ventilator. Four days passed, and the doctors told the family that it was time to make a decision about whether or not to take her off life support. Karen then lashed out at the surgeons in the conference room. Her grief turned to anger as they so nonchalantly talked about her sister's life. She told them they needed to have a little more concern and they needed to show more compassion for human life. Just to give them a small sample of how special her sister was, she informed them that she and her husband were ballroom dancers and had often performed in competition. The neurosurgeon, a woman, said, "I knew your sister was a ballroom dancer. I had seen them compete many times." The doctor had a passion for ballroom dancing as well. As the woman's husband and the doctor left the conference room that day, they began to dance in the halls of the hospital as a tribute to his wife. Those who can dance in the face of tragedy have truly experienced the grace of God.

There is a time for everything, and a season
for every activity under heaven:
A time to weep and time to laugh;
a time to mourn, and a time to dance.
Ecclesiastes 3:1,4

Day 51

The Narrow Gate

One Sunday night, during our weekly youth group meeting, several of our youth leaders had made other commitments, and I was responsible for teaching the lesson. After looking through one of our resource books, I decided on a lesson titled *Signs of the End Times*. I was sure this topic would stimulate good conversation from an already inquisitive group. We began reading various scriptures where Jesus revealed signs of the end times to his disciples and others who had gathered to hear him teach. The discussion was intense and the youth asked very difficult questions—some I could not answer. One example was, "Where is heaven?" This led us to a different topic—how does someone get to heaven? We continued to discuss the scriptures we were reading, and almost every child raised their hand with a comment or a question before the night was over.

There was one young girl there whom I did not remember seeing before. She sat quietly during the entire lesson, and eventually she got the courage to raise her hand to ask a question. I noticed a look of concern on her face when she asked about the narrow gate. She thought that the gate to heaven was physically narrow. If the end of the world came and there were thousands of people trying to get into heaven, she was afraid she would not have a chance to get in because of the narrow opening. I quickly explained that the scripture referring to the narrow gate meant that the way to heaven was narrow and there was only one way to get there—through Jesus Christ. The look on that young girl's face is something I will never forget. She looked as if the weight of the world suddenly lifted off her shoulders. I did not see her during any of our other youth meetings and cannot help but believe that she came that night for one reason—to open her heart to the truth. Being the one to deliver the message was indescribable.

"Enter through the narrow gate. For wide is the gate and broad is the road that leads to destruction, and many enter through it. But small is the gate and narrow the road that leads to life, and only a few find it."
Matthew 7:13–14

Day 52

The Phone Call

During the prayer time of our woman's Bible study, we all share our concerns and keep a written record of the people we want to lift in prayer during the week. This particular night's prayer time started much like any other night. Then one of the women in our Bible study began to share things that were obviously heavy on her heart. We were not quite sure of all the details, but she and her father had not spoken in four years, and she had not heard from her son in over a year. As she began to share a few more details with us, her lips began to quiver as she tried to share what was on her heart without losing total control of her emotions.

Her prayer request was the last one on our list, and our Bible study leader saw the need for us to have a group hug. We all went to the floor on our knees as we put our arms around each other's shoulders. We prayed for all the people whose names were mentioned, and we especially prayed for our broken-hearted Christian sister. We knew God was there with us as we could feel his presence in the room.

Each week we looked forward to Bible study, but one of the best parts was hearing the answers to our prayer requests. When we met the next week, our friend could not hold in her news and just started telling us about what kind of week she had and how our prayers had worked in her family. The Friday before had been her birthday, and the secretary at the school where she worked came to tell her she had a phone call. It was from her father. Even before she got to the phone, she asked God to be with the conversation. The healing process had begun as father and daughter began to make plans for the future.

If this were the only phone call she received this week, one would surely know that God had indeed answered our prayers. However, that was not the only phone call she received. The next Sunday was Mother's Day. She said she had not expected to hear from her son on her birthday, but it would be nice to hear from him on Mother's Day. Nevertheless, she felt the odds of that happening were slim to none. Then around 9:30 p.m., the phone rang that Sunday night. It was her son, and she immediately thanked God for this second miracle. God knows our hearts, and he mourns for us when our hearts are broken. Sometimes those are the times when we come closest to God because that is when we need him most.

My flesh and my heart may fail,
but God is the strength
of my heart and my portion forever.
Psalm 73:26

Day 53

The Plant

As I was walking back to my office one day, I spotted a plant on top of a trashcan. It looked like it needed water, and some of the leaves had started to turn yellow and brown. I assumed it was to be thrown away, but the person who left it there did not really want to put it in the trashcan. Maybe they were hoping someone would take it home and try to bring it back to life. I passed by that trash can for a couple of days, and when I realized that no one else was going to take the plant, I took it to my office.

It could have easily been discarded as a lost cause with no chance for survival, but I began to prune the dead leaves and nurture it back to health. As I pruned, I noticed a beautiful plant beginning to emerge. All it needed was the right person to take care of it and to know where it needed pruning. As I delicately trimmed back the unhealthy parts, I started to think that this is exactly what God does with us when we have "dead leaves or branches" in our lives that do not produce fruit. He knows exactly what to take out of our lives to make us a more-fruitful Christian. It may be one job ending so a better job can come along. It may be that he shuts a door to a path that you thought was the right decision, only to find that he opens a window to a better opportunity.

God is the perfect gardener, and Jesus is the True Vine to which we must stay connected, so he can prune us and help us be fruitful. We are the branches that produce Jesus' fruit on earth to promote the kingdom of heaven to all who will listen. Therefore, if you feel like some things have been happening to you that you do not understand, stop and look to see if you are being pruned. Jesus is probably preparing you for a more-bountiful harvest.

"I am the vine; you are the branches. If a man remains in me and I in him, he will bear much fruit; apart from me you can do nothing. If anyone does not remain in me, he is like a branch that is thrown away and withers; such branches are picked up, thrown into the fire and burned. If you remain in me and my words remain in you, ask whatever you wish, and it will be given you. This is to my Father's glory, that you bear much fruit, showing yourselves to be my disciples."
John 15:5–8

Day 54

The Snake in the Door

On a recent road trip, my Aunt Ruby had an experience with a snake. She had a pickup truck and a snake had made its way into the driver's side door hinge. She was running errands, had been getting in and out of the truck all morning, and had not noticed the snake. During one of her stops, a friend noticed what had happened. He calmly told her to slowly slide to the passenger side of the truck and get out. The man then proceeded to open the driver's side door and kill the snake.

What attracted me to this story was the fact that my aunt had been going about her daily routine and that snake had been just inches away from her the whole time without her noticing. The snake was very slick and sly, just like Satan is in our lives. He and his demons can be just as close as that snake was to my Aunt Ruby, and we may not even notice.

Sometimes it takes someone else looking at our lives to see Satan's mischievous ways. His way is conniving and devious. He can disguise himself as something good for a while before we notice that he is full of lies. We can count ourselves fortunate if we have friends who can help us avoid Satan's plan to interfere in our relationship with God and point out the dangers he presents in our lives. We have to keep our eyes and ears open to his constant attempts to deter us from our Christian walk.

Be self-controlled and alert. Your enemy the devil prowls around like a roaring lion looking for someone to devour. Resist him, standing firm in the faith, because you know that your brothers throughout the world are undergoing the same kind of sufferings.
1 Peter 5:8–9

Day 55

Thorns or Roses?

Roses are some of the most beautiful, fragrant flowers on earth. Anniversaries and weddings are often adorned with these stunning gifts of nature. My grandmother loved roses. She pruned, dusted, and nurtured her rosebushes to perfection. She had over seventy rose bushes in her yard and many times when she and my mother would visit me in college, she would bring a bouquet from her flower garden. Many Sundays she placed flowers in her church to glorify God and his beautiful creation.

Even though roses are beautiful and fragrant, they also have thorns. If you are not careful, you can get a painful prick from handling a rose carelessly. In Paul's second letter to the Corinthians, he talks about having a thorn in his side, which tormented him. He pleaded with God to take the thorn away. However, God denied his request, saying that he would be with him and his grace would be sufficient for any thorns he had to endure. I can attest to the fact that God does indeed supply enough grace to endure our thorns. Had it not been for some of the thorns in my life, I would probably be moving farther away from God instead of closer to him. Pain and suffering allow us the opportunity to call on him for comfort and strength. Adversity implores us to turn to God in times of despair. If we never had any unpleasant circumstances in our lives, how would we ever learn to depend on God? We would probably start to see ourselves as our own source of strength instead of the one True Source.

The beauty of the rose is that if you can endure the thorns long enough, with the grace of God you can become a stronger Christian with every painful prick. Another unexpected result that I have experienced is the fact that these encounters with the thorns will eventually produce beautiful, fragrant roses. These roses of life can come in many forms. You just have to be able to recognize them for what they are—precious gifts from God that teach us to be obedient to his Word.

Three times I pleaded with the Lord to take it away from me. But he said to me, "My grace is sufficient for you, for my power is made perfect in weakness."
2 Corinthians 12:8–9

Day 56

Up, Up, and Away

I had the opportunity to do something that I have never done before. Several other church members and I went to a local farm and gleaned sweet potatoes for people in need of food. We were fortunate enough to work with another local church and met others who also had a passion for helping others. When we started gathering the potatoes, one of the men from the other church came over to me and pointed at a potato that was partially visible. He said if I could see that much of a potato that there was probably a larger one underneath the dirt. I told him I had grown up on a farm and that one year, our entire acreage was planted with sweet potatoes. He kindly replied, "I guess I don't need to give you any more gleaning tips."

When I looked at that partially visible sweet potato, it reminded me that God's Word is the same way. If we dig deeper in the Word, we will find there are so many wonderful promises that God has for us. Many people probably know what John 3:16 says, and many others can recite the twenty-third psalm, but how many people really take the time to get into the scriptures and learn about all the good things he has in store for us?

We continued to glean potatoes, and after about three hours, we stopped to check on our progress. We had picked up over 2,500 pounds of potatoes in less than three hours! I was amazed at how much we had accomplished with so few people in such a short amount of time. The church we were gleaning with had a ritual of releasing balloons after completing a mission trip. These balloons had graphics on them that identified their church's mission team. When the gleaning was over, we stood and watched as the balloons floated slowly to the sky.

Later that afternoon, as I was returning home from the grocery store, I noticed a bunch of balloons on a road sign near my house. I said to my son, "They look like the balloons that were released today in the sweet potato field!" I told him that I just had to go back and get a closer look. To my surprise, they were the same! It is interesting to note that the field we were gleaning in was approximately twenty miles from where the balloons had landed. I wondered if God was trying to send me some kind of message with the balloons. As I traveled home, I silently listened for anything that he was trying to tell me, but nothing really seemed to materialize. The next day I passed by that same spot and I anxiously looked to see if the balloons were still there. They were there, but they were deflated and lying on the ground. Nevertheless, as I passed by I distinctly heard the voice of God. He was speaking to all those who had helped that day. He simply said, "Thank you."

*When you reap the harvest of your land, do not reap
to the very edges of your field or gather the
gleanings of your harvest. Do not go over
your vineyard a second time
or pick up the grapes that have fallen.
Leave them for the poor and the alien.*
Leviticus 19:9–10

Day 57

Van for Sale

A friend of mine had a used van she wanted to sell. She placed the van in a visible spot, hoping someone would see it and want to take it for a test drive. The van stayed in that spot for a couple of months with no one showing any interest in buying it. She then realized that she had not asked God to help her sell the van. She prayed for God to send someone who needed a good, used van.

During this same time, God was speaking to her to donate a large sum of money to a local cause. She prayed about this and even asked God if he was sure he wanted her to give that particular amount. Being an obedient servant, she went ahead and wrote the check that God had put on her heart to write. In just a couple of days, when she and her husband were at choir practice, a man stopped by to look at the van. He turned out to be a fine Christian man, and they were able to negotiate a deal that was agreeable to both parties. When the man paid my friend for her van, she noticed that the check covered what she was asking for the van, as well as more than enough to cover the donation she had recently made. God instructs us to pray about everything and to pray without ceasing. When we take that giant leap of faith, God graciously keeps his promises to meet our needs.

Do not be anxious about anything, but in

everything, by prayer and petition,
with thanksgiving, present your requests to God.
Philippians 4:6

Day 58

Walls of Water

One day I was contemplating the possible outcome of some prayers I had been praying. My body was going through the motions at my job, but my mind was on higher things. A prayer that I had prayed was answered, but it also created another situation about which I needed to pray. My mind started racing about how this particular turn of events would play out. I made a plan; then I changed my plan; then I went back to the first plan. Then I came to my senses and realized it is all God's plan to start with. All I have to do is walk down the path that he has made for me.

I started to think about times in the Bible when things looked dismal. The first image that came to my mind was when the Israelites left Egypt. They were traveling down the desert road that leads to the Red Sea when the Egyptians changed their minds about letting them go free and began to pursue them in great numbers. They became terrified and cried out to the Lord for help. The Israelites then changed their minds about leaving Egypt. They began to say it would have been better for them to remain slaves than face certain death in the desert. Moses responded with his usual, calm tone. "Don't be afraid," he said, "just be still." Then the Lord parted the Red Sea so the Israelites could escape and when the Egyptians followed in behind them, the walls of water collapsed and destroyed hundreds of the finest soldiers in Pharaoh's army. Then I began to think that if God could perform such an awesome miracle as parting the Red Sea, surely he could take care of my requests with no problem. All I have to do is not be afraid, be still, and let the power of Almighty God do the rest.

Then Moses stretched out his hand over the sea, and all that night the Lord drove the sea back with a strong east wind and turned it into dry land. The waters were divided, and the Israelites went through the sea on dry ground, with a wall of water on their right and on their left.
Exodus 14:21–22

Day 59

Where Is Esther?

*Dedicated to Bettie Dotson and Delores Hollowell,
Esther Mae's daughters.*

Let us face it; some books in the Bible are hard to
find. There are a couple of reasons for this.
Some of these books are just a few pages long and
are nestled between the larger books. Moreover,
these books are not usually the ones highlighted in
Sunday school curricula. When I have to look up a
verse in a lesser-known book, I first try to find it
without any help. However, many times I have to
resort to looking up the page number in the table of
contents.

When I am able to find one of the books on my
own, I can give credit to one person in particular. My
Aunt Esther Mae could be found at church every
time there was a service. When I was a small child,
we all went to church on Sunday night for Training
Union. My Aunt Esther Mae taught the class I was
in. One of the things we learned was the books of the
Bible. We were too young for deep, thought-provok-
ing discussions, but we got the basics. We learned
how to pray, we learned that Jesus loves us, and we
learned the books of the Bible.

My aunt had a unique way of teaching us how to
find the books of the Bible. She had a song for the
Old Testament books and a different song for the

New Testament books. We would sing these songs while we colored or while we were cutting out figures for the felt board. After all these years, I still hum those songs in my head when I am looking for Leviticus, 1 Chronicles, Colossians, or James. I begin to turn the page, and I can hear my Aunt Esther Mae's voice singing those books of the Bible. Because of this, she will always be a wonderful memory each time I am searching for one of those hard-to-find books. If you are looking for one of those hard-to-find books and you ask one day, "Where is Esther?" I would say, "She's in heaven, probably helping some of the children learn their books of the Bible."

"Whoever welcomes one of these little children in
my name welcomes me,
and whoever welcomes me does not welcome
me but the one who sent me."
Mark 9:37

Day 60

You Reap What You Sow

My father is a yard sale addict. He used to buy a wide variety of items, but recently he has resorted to purchasing musical instruments. It does not matter if anyone in the family can play it or not. He just feels like he is on a "mission" to rescue these instruments and get them into the hands of someone who can play. This one particular Saturday my father was unable to locate any local yard sales so he ventured to the next nearest town. He saw a small sign on a mailbox that said, "Yard Sale." He would have missed the sign if he had not been looking closely.

My father stopped to see what items this family had to offer. He spotted a saxophone and he asked the woman how much she wanted for the instrument. She told him she would sell it for one hundred dollars. My father had one hundred and twenty dollars in his pocket and he gave her the money without hesitation. He had a friend who played the saxophone and my dad thought he could add it to his collection.

He left in search of other yard sales. When he could not find any potential prospects, he returned to the house where he had bought the saxophone. The woman asked if he saw anything else he would like to have and he responded, "I've almost spent all of my cantaloupe money and I really can't afford to buy much more." When she heard this she quickly asked,

"Are you from Rocky Hock where they grow those good cantaloupes?" He said, "Yes I am." Rocky Hock is a small community in northeastern North Carolina known for growing many varieties of produce. Because the land is sandy, it is well suited for growing watermelons and cantaloupes. The next statement out of the woman's mouth fell on unbelieving ears. She said, "I will give you everything left in the house if you just bring me six cantaloupes." My father was not sure how to respond, but he agreed thinking that there probably was not much left anyway. Upon entering the house, he could not believe his eyes. The items left included a washer and dryer, dishwasher, and a stove. My brother was in the process of remodeling my grandparent's house and my father immediately knew where the appliances would be going. As he tried to comprehend the events of the morning, he thought to himself, "I think I'll give her twelve cantaloupes instead of six."

He went home to tell my mother what had happened. She could hardly believe her ears, but she could understand it. My father is one of the most unselfish people I have ever met and he will give his family, as well as strangers, anything that they need even if it means he has to go without. My mother just figured that this woman had returned to him all those years of giving.

My father was about to go and collect the twelve cantaloupes when the man he worked for came by to give him what was left from the mornings' market. When you take off a "load of cantaloupes," it usually means there are hundreds and sometimes thousands in a trailer. The man told my father he had sold almost all of his cantaloupes and he just wanted to bring the remaining ones to him. The number of cantaloupes left was twelve!

Remember this: Whoever sows sparingly
will also reap sparingly,
and whoever sows generously
will also reap generously.
II Corinthians 9:6

Printed in the United States
37090LVS00002B/1-195

9 781597 814072